THE WINDRUSH HISTORY

TWENTIETH

Other titles in the same series

Anti-Semitism by Roberto Finzi

Castro and Cuba by Angelo Trento

Crisis in the Middle East by François Massoulié

Gandhi and India by Gianni Sofri

Hitler and Nazism by Enzo Collotti

Mussolini and Fascism by Marco Palla

GABRIELE RANZATO

THE SPANISH CIVIL WAR

A CENTURY IN FOCUS

Translated by Janet Sethre Paxia

THE WINDRUSH PRESS • GLOUCESTERSHIRE

First published in Great Britain by
The Windrush Press in 1999
Little Window, High Street
Moreton-in-Marsh
Gloucestershire GL56 0LL
Tel: 01608 652012
Fax: 01608 652125
Email: windrush@windrushpress.com
Web site www.windrushpress.com

This edition of *The Spanish Civil War* is published by arrangement
with Giunti Gruppo Editoriale and Casterman Editions.

British Library Cataloguing in Publication Data
A catalogue record for this book is available from the British Library

ISBN 1 900624 31 1

Typeset by Archetype IT Ltd, web site: www.archetype-it.com
Printed and bound in Italy by Giunti Gruppo Editoriale

Source of the documents and photographs is the
Archives Giunti/DR unless otherwise credited.

Cover picture: Republican militia marching through the streets of Madrid in 1936

Contents

THE SPANISH CIVIL WAR

Chapter 1

SPAIN AT THE CENTER OF THE WORLD

JULY 1936: A GROUP OF SPANISH OFFICERS REBEL AGAINST THE REPUBLICAN GOVERNMENT. AT FIRST, IT SEEMS LIKE ONE OF THE MANY *PRONUNCIAMIENTOS* CHARACTERIZING SPANISH HISTORY. INSTEAD, IT IS ONLY THE BEGINNING OF A LONG CIVIL WAR.

In the mid-1930s, after languishing at the margins of history for more than a century, Spain became the center of world attention. The governments of many other countries, powers old and new, became involved in the Spanish crisis: England, France, Germany, Italy and the Soviet Union all intervened and clashed with one another. And a great number of private citizens from around the world also found themselves emotionally drawn into the conflict and compelled to choose sides. In a way, the situation was a throwback to the dramas of the nineteenth century, when – in Italy and Greece, for example – men were drawn into combat by the force of their convictions; then, too, volunteers had poured in to fight for the liberty and independence of countries foreign to them.

But this time the phenomenon exploded in the magnified forms of the twentieth century, on the stage of world history and mass society. Men of all social conditions – though mostly of the working class – hastened to Spain: from France in particular, but also from Poland, Germany, Italy, England, the United States, and about 50 other countries. Many of them crossed the border after following tortuous and clandestine paths, often defying the hostility of their own governments. Some of them knew how to use weapons, some had fought in the First World War; but many, especially among the intellectuals, possessed little or no military training, and were armed only by their enthusiasm.

What drove these (mostly) men to abandon their

From the top of the Ochandiano church belltower, a group of Republican soldiers guard the streets leading to Bilbao. After breaking out in July 1936, in the wake of the army's failed coup d'état against the Republic, the Spanish Civil War would end in late March 1939, with the entry of Franco's troops into Madrid.

homes and travel long distances, often in trying conditions, in order to face the dangers and suffering of war in an unknown country? In the nineteenth century, it had been the political ideal of liberalism that had inspired volunteer soldiers in many a war of independence; now, it was a international ideal that led such combatants in Spain: the defense of democracy and communism, which many of the volunteers considered to be the highest form of democracy. The enemy was nothing less than fascism. That peninsula lying at the edge of Europe, the home – in a collective imagination conditioned by exotic clichés – of the matador and the flamenco dancer, wild passions and the Inquisition, thus became the theater of the first military conflict between the great ideologies and political choices of the twentieth century: liberal democracy, fascism, and communism.

***A** poster by the Catalan painter, Joan Miró (1893–1983) in support of the Spanish Republic.*

One of the volunteers, the Italian intellectual, Carlo Rosselli, perfectly grasped the importance of the clash; he saw the Spanish conflict as the "first battlefield." In a speech broadcast by Radio Barcelona and directed to his fellow countrymen, he pronounced a sentence destined to become famous: "Today in Spain; tomorrow in Italy." Of course, Italy was not the only country implicated in Spain's war. Despite the near-sighted politics of "appeasement" (the search for peace at any price) practiced by the democratic powers (England, France and, marginally, United States), when confronted with the aggressive politics of the Fascist powers (Germany, Italy, Japan), the end of the Spanish Civil War preceded by only a few months the beginning of the Second World War, in which, beyond the concrete interests of the warring nations, the triumph or defeat of conflicting political ideologies was at stake above all. In fact, we may well consider the Spanish Civil War to be a rehearsal for the Second World War – and not only in terms of military strategies and developments.

July 1936: A Nearly-aborted Coup d'État

What events, then, justified such an influx of volunteer fighters? What had actually happened in Spain? On July 17, 1936, according to a pre-established plan, officers took command by force of the military garrison in Morocco and rebelled against the legitimate government of the Republic. This government was supported by the Popular Front, a coalition of democratic parties that had won the elections during the preceding February. In the three days that followed, a great number of military units also mutinied in Spain itself, attempting to take control of vast areas of the country and achieve unity among themselves. The head of the Republican government, Santiago Casares Quiroga, proved incapable of finding a solution, whether by opposing or compromising with the rebels, and so he resigned (his reactionary intentions were actually quite apparent, despite his vague proclamations to the contrary). Nor did his moderate successor, Diego Martínez Barrio, manage to create any of the conditions necessary to dissuade the rebels from their intentions. In a telephone message, the main perpetrator of the coup,

Arms are handed out in the zone still controlled by the government. The decision to arm civilians was made after much hesitation on the part of José Giral's government. The decision was seen as an extreme measure necessary to oppose the military coup.
© Publifoto

***J**osé Giral was called to the government after Casares Quiroga's resignation, and Martínez Barrio's failure to mediate. A member of the Left Republican Party, Giral was an important ally of Manuel Azaña.*

General Emilio Mola, who was leading the rebels from a headquarters in Navarra, refused to compromise with Barrio. He refused even to propose conditions for surrender, thus making clear not only the inevitability of a cruel war, but his embracing of it.

The rebel forces had certainly anticipated partial failures, and with them, the need for armed confrontation with those army units that had remained loyal to the government. But they surely had not foreseen the nearly total failure of their coup d'état. Three days after its beginning, the rebels were in dire straits.

In the principal cities of Spain – Madrid, Barcelona, Bilbao, Valencia, Málaga – as well as in the richest and most highly industrialized areas of the country – Catalunya, the Basque country, Asturias – the rebellion had been quenched. The new head of the Republican government, José Giral, had allowed the distribution of weapons to the people, and these popular forces had defeated the rebel troops, which were either poorly led (as in Barcelona) or incapable of taking the initiative (as in Madrid). The rebels retained control of the mountainous zones of Navarra, half of Aragon, vast stretches of rural Castile, marginal Galicia, and much of Andalusia, including its capital, Seville. This was the only big city to fall into the hands of the coup forces, thanks to the audacity of Gonzalo Queipo de Llano, perhaps the toughest and cruelest of the rebel generals.

Even seen from a strictly military perspective, the *alzamiento* (insurrection), as the military forces triumphantly called their national mutiny, seemed doomed to failure. At least half of the military regulars had remained loyal in those areas that were controlled by government forces and, at least in theory, they constituted a striking force equal to that of the rebels. The officers, too, were divided evenly between the two zones, but their degree of reliability was not: in the rebel zone, hardly any officers defected, while in the Republican zone, perhaps due to an excess of diffidence toward the professional military forces, a relatively small number of experienced commanders

***R**ight, Moors of the African army near University City in Madrid. In order to weaken the Francoist army, the Anarchists suggested that the Republican government grant independence to Spanish Morocco.The obvious harm that this move might cause to Spain's relations with France and England led the Popular Front to refuse.*

A BREAKDOWN OF THE MILITARY FORCES

A few days after the military coup, 29 provincial capitals and an area of close to 89,000 square miles were in the hands of the rebels, as opposed to the 21 provincial capitals and the 104,000 square miles remaining with the government of the Republic. On the basis of this subdivision, we can calculate that the Republic could avail itself of 46,000 men in the metropolitan infantry, while the rebels had 44,000. This is a very rough estimate, because in the days of the coup (it was midsummer) about 14,000 soldiers of the Republican zone and 13,000 from the Nationalist one were on leave, and we do not know to what extent those soldiers returned to their posts. In theory, the Republic, which controlled the most important urban centers, could avail itself of a greater number of law enforcement officers than the rebels (42,000 as opposed to 25,000), including: the Guardia Civil – a fundamentally rural police corps, though present in the cities in consistent numbers; the Guardias de Asalto – a corps created expressly for the defense of the Republic; and the Carabineros – frontier and financial police. The men of these bodies were better trained than the enlisted soldiers, but their uncertain loyalties and their need to continue to carry out policing functions severely limited their capacity to join the Republican forces at the battlefront. The Guardia Civil, in particular, had often rebelled against the Republican authorities. Perhaps the best known episode involved the courageous resistance of much of the Jaén provincial corps, which was under siege from July of 1936 until May of 1937 in the sanctuary of Santa María de la Cabeza.

The breakdown of officers turns out to be even more significant. Theoretically, based on the territorial division, the combating sides almost equally shared 15,000 army officers. But the radical difference was that while almost all others, apart from some executed by the rebels, most were removed from their posts, jailed or somehow kept at the margins of the war. The breakdown of the youngest officers, many of whom had been won over by right-wing ideas, was just as unfavorable to the Republic; in total, the officers fighting in its army never exceeded 2,500–3,000 men.

All of which makes it easy to

those in the Nationalist zone were loyal to the rebels, in the other zone, fewer than twenty percent of the officers fought in the Republican army. Of the seventeen generals in the highest posts of command, for example, just five rebelled (Franco, Cabanellas, Queipo de Llano, Fanjui and Goded, of which the latter two were executed in the Republican zone), but only two (Riquelme and La Cerda) fought for the Republic. Of the 73 brigade generals, 22 rebelled, and only ten fought in the Republican army. Of the see why the role played by the African army was so decisive. Aligned completely on the side of the rebels, it boasted 47,000 men (of whom just 13,000 were actually African) who were particularly skillful in frontal assaults and hand-to-hand combat. The airlift and naval aid from the Fascist powers in favor of the Nationalists weakened the effectiveness of Republican control over most of the navy and air force – which were, at any rate, rather poorly-equipped and poorly-trained. ■

remained to lead the war operations.

The rebel forces were also decidedly favored by the fact that they could command nearly all the African army (approximately 47,000 men). This Moroccan branch of the Spanish army was tempered by tough discipline and by actual war experience, and flanked by the *Regulares*, a particularly aggressive corps of Moroccan troops led by the most skilled officers, the *Africanistas*, who were a true military aristocracy. One of its most notable members was Francisco Franco, the youngest (44 years old) and most capable of all the generals of the Spanish army. But these forces faced the difficulty of moving from Morocco to the mainland, a problem made particularly serious since 80 percent of the Navy had remained loyal to the Republic and held control of the Strait of Gibraltar; similarly, the commercial and military air forces were almost entirely under government control. Without the African army, the rebel generals' future was uncertain; they were dislocated on strips of land disconnected from each other;

After landing on the peninsula with the help of an Italo-German airlift, the Nationalist army pushed north along the Portuguese border, planning to attack Madrid. By the end of October, Franco was able to wage a battle for the capital.

THE SPANISH FRONT IN 1936

what they had anticipated as a rapid and final coup had failed, and they now faced the prospect of a long and wearing war.

Foreign Intervention

When three years later, in May of 1939, General Franco undertook to celebrate his civil war victory with a military parade, the march opened with a battalion of "black shirts" from the Italian expedition corps, and closed with pilots from the Condor Legion, the German air squadron that had participated in the most important war operations in the air. Such a symbolic placement was more than just a sign of gratitude for help received; it was an acknowledgment of the fact that, had the two Fascist powers not intervened, not only would there have been no victory for Franco, but there might have been no civil war at all. From the very beginning, indeed, their intervention was decisive.

As early as July 25, 1936, a week after the coup, Hitler welcomed to the Wagnerian festival at Bayreuth a delegation that had come to further the cause of the Nationalists, as the rebel side quickly came to be called, and presented them with a series of Junkers transport planes. And three days later, German planes began to set up an airlift between Morocco and the peninsula, assisted by a number of Savoia 81 planes sent over by Mussolini. In little more than a week, it thus became possible to transport 14,000 men, the first large contingent of the African army, across the Strait of Gibraltar. Later, more troops moved via the sea, thanks to the presence of German warships, which intimidated the Republican fleet. The Republicans were already incapable of creating any efficient blockade, due to obstacles set up by the authorities in Tangiers and by the American oil companies, which refused to carry fuel across the Strait.

Once it had reached the peninsula, the African army, commanded by General Franco, began to advance rapidly along Spain's western border. Led by Colonels Asensio and Yagüe, the Nationalist forces edged along the friendly borders of dictator Salazar's Portugal.

Within a single week, the African army penetrated about 125 miles into Spain, encountering little or no

Francisco Franco as a cadet at the military academy. Born on December 4, 1892, he was not admitted to the naval academy, where the members of his family had traditionally served; he had to settle for the less prestigious infantry. In spite of his mediocre record at the academy, thanks to his performance during the war of the Rif he had a brilliant career, which raised him to the rank of general at the age of only 33 years. Appointed head of the chiefs of staff by the War Minister and right-wing leader, Gil Robles, Franco would later be distanced from the Popular Front government by being appointed military governor of the Canary Islands.

resistance; it occupied Estremadura, conquered Badajoz after violent combat, moved up the Tagus valley and settled in at Talavera de la Reina, from where it hoped to attack Madrid, which lay about 100 miles away.

The Republican government was unable to organize a quick resistance. Although there were plenty of men willing to fight, the Republicans lacked the capacity to rapidly reorganize an army that had been amputated at several points, an army forced to do without sufficient leadership from an officer corps which, even if not openly involved in the rebellion, could no longer inspire much trust. It is true that the militias, the popular troops organized by political parties and labor unions, managed to cut off the southbound rebel army on the Sierra; but danger still threatened from the south, where the enemy's better-oiled war machine was in full function.

At this point the Republican government hoped to gain strength from its international legitimacy, and thus procure weapons that would compensate for its operative inferiority (from the beginning, weapons had been scarce on both sides). For their part, the rebels had already received consistent help from the Fascist powers, and this fact encouraged the Republicans to look

Militiamen engaged in battle with the rebel army on the outskirts of Madrid. After the coup d'état had been defeated with the help of the people, the Republican government still had great difficulty facing the coup forces' troops. The Republicans hoped to make up for their army's lack of experience and reliable commanders by throwing political militias into the skirmish. These were supposed to compensate for their poor military training with their enthusiasm.

for military assistance from the democratic powers, above all from France, since there, too, a Popular Front government had just come to power (in April 1936).

The intervention by Germany and Italy, however, as well as events developing in the two zones, had changed the shape and implications of the Spanish drama. Now any action taken by democratic governments to bring concrete assistance to Republican Spain implied competition with the Fascist powers and threatened to endanger an international equilibrium that was already extremely precarious after the German rearmament of the Rhineland and the Italian invasion of Ethiopia. The fear was that intervention might drag nations into a war for which they were unprepared. Nevertheless, world public opinion viewed the support the Fascist powers were giving to a military rebellion against a democratically elected government as an egregious attack against democracy.

In the face of this contradiction, which created particular difficulties for Léon Blum's French government, French and British diplomats worked out a policy of "non-intervention." In the pact of August 2, both countries promised absolute neutrality in the conflict and prohibited the dispatch of weapons to Spain. During the month that followed, all the major powers signed the agreement, except the United States, which, however, acted according to the criteria of the pact. Obviously, such a pact was extremely harmful to the Spanish Republic: in the first place because its legitimate government had been put on the same level with a power that had no right to international recognition; and in the second place, because the accord was put into effect after the adversary had already received generous assistance. At the end of August, when Germany, too, agreed to the pact, not only had the transfer of the African army been completed, but important consignments of weapons had been sent in ships to Spain, and further loads were already on their way from German ports.

Once the Fascist powers had intervened, the significance of the Spanish conflict pushed another international power onto the stage: the Soviet Union, whose ideological inspiration was antithetical to fascism.

The man advancing
is a strange soldier.
He comes from the
East, he rides no
horse.
His hands are
calloused, his face is
suntanned:
He is the most glorious
of all warriors.
He wears no plumes,
no golden stripes,
but on his cap and
engraved in his heart,
he bears a crossed
hammer and sickle.

– Song of the Garibaldi battalion

The "homeland of Socialism" was at a turning point in its history. Stalin was about to complete his final triumph over all his domestic adversaries and set up an absolute dictatorship, but his international policy had suffered a number of failures. The prospects for exporting the revolution had declined; the Soviets now took refuge in the idea of "socialism in a single country." This formula required the USSR to seek peace, alliances and assurances in the face of possible aggression from Nazi Germany. In the end, the Spanish drama represented a dilemma for the Soviets just as it did for the Western democracies. Those sympathizing with the international communist movement could not remain indifferent to the fate of the Republic. But neither could one jeopardize an entire policy – of which the Popular Fronts promoted by the Communist International were only one part – meant to strengthen bonds with the Western powers.

***A** demonstration in support of the Spanish Republic, in Paris. As early as August 1936, groups of volunteers spontaneously headed to Spain from France, which was led by a Popular Front government as well. The great majority of Italian volunteers also arrived from France, where they had emigrated as early as the 1920s to find work, or for political reasons.*
© Publifoto

In any case, it quickly became obvious that Stalin gave preference to the need to help the Spanish Republic. He did so even at the risk of jeopardizing his relationship with the West, perhaps because of the growing revolutionary developments in the Republican zone. These developments gave credibility to the rebels' accusations: a communist revolution was about to break out, they said, in the face of which the *alzamiento* was only a necessary, preventive action. The same events awakened the concern of conservative forces within the democratic countries. In the early phase, however, assistance from the USSR was not directly military (the first Soviet weapons did not reach Spain until early October). Instead, it was directed at moving international public opinion in favor of the Republic, and at encouraging many of the volunteer fighters, organizing them and converting them into an efficient instrument of war: the International Brigades.

In this enterprise, the Soviet Union could avail itself of a highly efficient instrument, the Communist International, an organization almost entirely under its control, now that the international movement had accepted the slogan of "socialism in a single country." The antifascist movement of solidarity with Republican

Miguel de Unamuno (1864–1936) at first sided with the military. But faced with its excesses and the prospect of a bloody civil war ending in a fascist dictatorship, he publicly disowned the coup forces' actions. In a celebrated speech given at the University of Salamanca, he warned Franco and his supporters, "You will win, but you will not convince."

INTELLECTUALS TAKE SIDES

The civil war also forced intellectuals and artists to make choices. The Republic saw most of them rush to its side. At the head of a long list, we can find the names of the poets Antonio Machado, Rafael Alberti, and Miguel Hernández. But Spain saw other valorous sons opt for the other side: Manuel Machado, Antonio's brother; and the Catalans, Eugeni D'Ors and Josep Pla. Some of the most widely respected figures of Spanish culture, such as José Ortega y Gasset, Pérez de Ayala and Pio Baroja, repelled by the violence in the Republican area, adhered to the rebel cause with some reservations, but then were unable to live in the clerico-fascist environment of the Nationalist zone, and moved abroad. One famous case was that of the writer and philosopher Miguel de Unamuno, who, after supporting the military insurrection, disowned it in a public speech that cost him his post as rector of the University of Salamanca.

The mobilization of international culture was enormous, and overwhelmingly in favor of the Republic. The most famous writers and poets who supported the Republic include: Malraux, Prévert, Spender, Faulkner, Hemingway, Brecht, Mann, and Neruda. The cinema, too, came out in favor of the Republican cause, including such Hollywood actors and directors as Joan Crawford, Bette Davis, John Ford, and King Vidor.

The choice of so many famous and respected individuals to support the Republic markedly influenced international public opinion. Perhaps the most important initiative was the Conference of Antifascist Writers, which was held in itinerant form in July of 1937, between Valencia, Madrid and Barcelona, ending in a large public assembly in Paris. On that occasion, Bertolt Brecht pointed his finger at the threat implied by the Spanish war – a threat against culture itself, he called it. He ended his speech with a call to arms: "Culture has been defended for a long time – too long a time – only with spiritual weapons, while attacked with material ones.... It must be defended with material weapons." ■

Spain was naturally spontaneous. All the nations of democratic Europe, as well as the United States, saw a rapid growth of initiatives, meetings, collections of goods for humanitarian aid, and declarations of principle by intellectuals and other people of culture. But such spontaneity was stimulated, channeled, structured, widened; in short, rendered more efficient, by a network of organizations such as the International Committee for Aid to the Spanish People, the Committee for

THE INTERNATIONAL BRIGADES

The first nucleus of volunteers destined to form the International Brigades arrived from Marseilles in early October 1936, at Alicante, on board the *Ciudad de Barcelona*. From there the men were transferred to Albacete, a military training base and also a point of political control, led by the tough, suspicious old French revolutionary, André Marty, along with the Italians Luigi Longo, general inspector, and Giuseppe Di Vittorio, central political commissary – all of whom were members of their respective Communist parties. Their model was that of the Red Army, with its military commander and political commissary; but although the enrollment, organization and training of the Brigades was governed by the Communist International, not all those who fought in them were members of the party. In fact, in some of the units, such as the Italian Garibaldi battalion, Communists did not even constitute a majority. Among the non-communist combatants, one could find socialist antifascist militants such as Pietro Nenni, alongside many young people who were inspired, in part, by the spirit of adventure, such as Esmond Romilly, Winston Churchill's eighteen-year-old nephew. During the war, seven brigades were organized, each divided into three or four battalions, mostly with a national base. The first to enter the battle was the 11th Brigade, named for Hans Beimler, the German political commissary (who was among the first to be killed in Spain); it was composed of the Edgar André German battalion, the French-Belgian Commune de Paris, and the Polish Dabrowski battalion. The International Brigades – among which the most distinguished were the Garibaldi, the Marseillaise, the Yugoslav Dimitrov and the American Lincoln – participated in all the most important battles of the war: the battles of Madrid, Jarama, Guadalajara, Brunete, Teruel, and the great Ebro offensive. Some of their commanders, such as the Rumanian, Kléber, and the Hungarian, Lukacz, became legendary. If we consider the average ratio of combatants to casualties, the many losses suffered by the Brigades – about 10,000 dead – give credibility to the scholar Andreu Castells' estimate of 60,000 "internationals" who participated in the war. ■

Aid to the Victims of Fascism, and the International Red Rescue, whose efforts were sustained, more or less discreetly, by the Communist International.

Solidarity thus spread, and the inaction of the democratic governments fell under heavy criticism; France, in particular, was squeezed between the urgings of public opinion (which was largely consonant with the government) and the need to act in harmony with its British ally. Swayed by the climate of solidarity, France decided to follow through with the dispatch of airplanes to the Republic – a total of 50 all told – until August 10, when the calls for adherence to the policy of "non-intervention" grew louder.

Even in the case of volunteer fighters, the organizational phase sustained by the International was preceded by a wave of spontaneity. French, Belgians, and Italian and German antifascist exiles were the first to rush to Spain, especially to Barcelona where, poorly armed, they improvised columns of combatants and marched off to the Aragon front, without any well-defined military strategy. After this initial phase, which relied on the spontaneity of militia troops organized by political parties and labor unions, at the same time the Republican armed forces themselves were "re-militarized," the foreign volunteers were recruited through various organizations that were controlled by the International. These organizations were mostly located in France, which was the headquarters of both *Paix et Liberté* and *Amis de l'URSS*. These organizations channeled foreign volunteers to Albacete, in the region of La Mancha. The volunteers were then trained (intensely at times, and at others, hardly at all) and placed in the ranks of the International Brigades.

Two soldiers of the International Brigades, in photos taken by Robert Capa and Agustí Centelles. Help from the international volunteers not only had symbolic value, but also considerable military importance, since many volunteers had experience in the First World War.

The Battle of Madrid

The contribution of the International Brigades was to be of extreme importance during all the main phases of the civil war, above all in the defense of Madrid, where in early November they were baptized by fire. Their efforts were decisive, not so much because of their military experience (many combatants had none), but because of the intensity of their struggle, which was sustained by strong ideological convictions. The presence of the volunteers reassured the people of Madrid. The International Brigades thus collaborated in defeating what had seemed, in the mid-autumn, an imminent victory for the rebels.

Indeed, the advancement of Franco's army had proceeded ceaselessly. It had certainly been abetted by the military aid – planes, cannons, rifles – that Germany and Italy had sent during the last ten days of August, despite their declared "non-intervention." At the same time, the Fascist powers had been encouraged in their aid efforts by Franco's victories, which were due above all to his adversaries' lack of military prowess. The Fascist powers foresaw an easy victory, which they hoped to exploit later on, by taking credit for it. France's and England's inertia in the face of the Fascist violation of the non-intervention pact – which they themselves had, on the contrary, rigidly respected – ended up weakening their position, since it encouraged the aggressiveness of the Fascist powers. But we must remember that in the early months, a rapid defeat of the Republic had seemed probable, so that any other line of conduct must have seemed imprudent.

***M**ost members of the International Brigades came from European countries, but some volunteers traveled from other continents to come to Spain's aid – particularly from North America.*

After observing the democratic powers' passivity in the face of an imminent rebel victory over Madrid, the Soviet Union decided to break out of the limbo with direct intervention, attempting to compensate the Republic for the military aid the Nationalists had already received from Italy and Germany. On October 4, the first Soviet ship loaded with weapons anchored at the port of Cartagena. By the end of the month, "Katyusha" Tupolev bombers attacked the rebel airports, while powerful T–26 tanks appeared in

Sesena, opposing the Nationalists' advance against Madrid.

Hitler and Mussolini accepted the challenge, immediately deciding to increase aid to the Nationalist camp and to officially recognize its government. The Fuhrer sent the Condor Legion to Spain, where German military advisors were already in operation; this Legion would constitute the essential nucleus of the Nationalist air force. Enjoying considerably more autonomy than the Spanish units, the Legion required the presence of about 5,000 men in order to operate (but since the soldiers rotated regularly, actually about 30,000 Germans ended up fighting in Spain). Beginning with its first military action that November, in the battle of Madrid, the Legion tested fighting and bombing techniques that Germany would later apply during the Second World War.

Following this new development, in which Spain became the battleground for a confrontation between the Soviet Union and the Fascist powers, the political and ideological characteristics of the countries sponsoring the combatants were imposed on the two sides. The defense of the Republic and the defense of

During a pause in the fighting, rations are distributed behind Republican lines at the Madrid front. Franco's attack on the capital represented an attempt to end the conflict rapidly. In spite of the optimistic predictions, shared by his international allies, the battle, which began in November 1936, ended in solemn defeat.
© Publifoto

democracy no longer seemed to coincide. From the world's point of view, fascism and communism were fighting each other, just outside Madrid. And while the democracies continued to sympathize with the fate of the besieged Republic, they were also worried by the growing influence that the Soviet Union was able to exercise over the Spanish government, because of the aid it offered.

***R**epublican militia in defense of Madrid. Franco's hopes for the fall of Madrid were nourished by the fact that during the first days of the offensive, the Nationalist troops had reached the city center and cut University City in two.*

The defense of Madrid is a historical fact that has become a legend even in today's world. In early November, the capital seemed lost: defending it seemed a hopeless battle. Franco's army, led by General Varela, had arrived in the city. The particular configuration of Madrid, whose historical and directional center is at the periphery of the urban nucleus, caused the battlefront to lie less than a mile away from the heart of the city. With surprise and admiration, foreign observers saw soldiers and militia fighters stop off in the coffee shops of the Gran Vía or the Puerta del Sol, before rushing to the front. The city suffered from numerous terrorist bombings – here, too, a bloody precedent to those of the world war – and the government, headed since September by the socialist Largo Caballero, abandoned it, turning over its defense to a *Junta* directed by General Miaja.

"Madrid will be the tomb of fascism," they said, and antifascist newspapers all over the world repeated it. "*No pasaran*" (They shall not pass) became the motto for Madrileños defending their city, and for all of Republican Spain. These slogans and words of hope became integral to the epic of the Spanish war. They encouraged the people, gave them determination; they magnetized international solidarity, and nurtured heroic episodes. But by now the last line of defense had been reached, on the bridges over the Manzanares and in the University zone, where people were shooting at each other from one department to the next. The Republican army, which was still being re-militarized after the phase of popular militias, resisted the enemy attack, but it was near collapse.

Then, onto the field marched the International Brigades, who notably strengthened the Republic's defense, and overhead flew Soviet airplanes, whose consistent intervention matched the enemy's fighter planes and bombers.

Between November 16 and 17, Franco unleashed a powerful offensive in response, including the furious bombardment that was masterfully described by André Malraux in his novel, *L'Espoir*. People fought from house to house, in the Hospital Clínico, in the House of Velázquez, in the gardens of the Moncloa Palace. But the Nationalist avant-garde, after succeeding in breaking through the Republican defense into an area bounded by the Franceses and Segovia Bridges, was closed into a sort of cul-de-sac from which it was unable to free itself until the end of the war. A week later, with his army decimated by the weak offensive, Franco had disappointed his powerful allies' easy enthusiasm. He was forced to give up his attempt to take the capital with a frontal attack. For him, the battle of Madrid was lost.

Nationalist soldiers at the Madrid front. By the end of November, Franco had to give up a direct attack on the capital. From then on, all the battles that took place in the center of the country were really attempts to reach Madrid.

Chapter 2

INCUBATION

DEMOCRACY, FASCISM, COMMUNISM. FROM THE PERSPECTIVE OF WORLD HISTORY, THESE WERE THE IDEOLOGIES, POLITICAL DOCTRINES, AND VALUES FOUGHT FOR IN SPAIN. BUT WERE THINGS QUITE THE SAME FROM A SPANISH PERSPECTIVE? WERE THE SAME VALUES AND FORCES AT THE ROOT OF THE SPANISH CIVIL WAR?

In the first place, let us take a look at what sparked the war: a military uprising against democratic institutions. The country was not taken over by any Fascist party, but – as we have seen – assaulted by a military coup d'état. This event belongs fully to the Spanish tradition of *pronunciamientos*, or intervention by the military in the political life of the country.

Militarism and Fascism

Indeed, from 1814 (when General Espoz y Mina made the first *pronunciamiento* against the restoration of absolutism by Ferdinand VII) to 1936, we can count all of 52 attempts at *pronunciamiento*. Even the *alzamiento* of 1936 had been preceded in 1932 by an aborted monarchical *pronunciamiento* by General Sanjurjo, who was then forced to take refuge abroad. The Republic itself had been preceded by seven years of the military dictatorship of General Primo de Rivera, who had seized power with a coup d'état in 1923. Interestingly, the *pronunciamiento* was not only a right-wing, anti-democratic method; in fact, in the nineteenth century, and in the twentieth as well, during Primo de Rivera's dictatorship, three attempts at a military coup d'état involved democratic forces. It was as if, in some

A *1933 demonstration by commercial and industrial employees in Barcelona. The years preceding the outbreak of the civil war were characterized by a radicalization of social conflicts, which were partly due to the worsening of the economic crisis after 1929. Suffocated during Primo de Rivera's dictatorship, social tension now exploded with great violence.*

© Sergi i Octavi Centelles

Face to the sun, with

a new shirt –

yesterday you

embroidered it in red.

I shall find death if it

comes,

and shall never see

you again.

– Falange song

way, military force were the powerful arm of a political party.

Even the coup of July 1936, although it had a clearly reactionary nature, failed to manifest a well-delineated ideological configuration. The confused terminology characterizing the rebel generals' first public messages was not just an expedient meant to confuse people's ideas, but actually reflected a real lack of political coordination. In his first proclamation, Franco spoke of restoring the values of the French Revolution. The *Junta de Defensa*, the rebels' first organizing body, was headed by the Masonic Republican, General Cabanellas; he, rather cryptically, declared that the "particular ideologies" of everyone would be respected, but that "political partisanship" would not be tolerated. During the early weeks, the Count of Rodezno, a supporter of the coup, complained of the generals' absolute "lack of political orientation."

The rebels seemed to be fundamentally apolitical, guided only by a love of technology (Franco's first government was called "Junta Técnica") and military hierarchy. In fact, that Franco prevailed over Mola, who had participated much more actively in the conspiracy, was clearly due to the fact that

Franco had a higher rank in the army.

In Spain there was an authentic Fascist party, the Falange, founded by José Antonio, the son of the ex-dictator, Primo de Rivera. But although it was intensely combative, the Falange was a small minority: founded in 1933, three years later it could boast no more than 10,000 militants. In the elections of February 1936, José Antonio, leading an independent list of candidates from a National Bloc uniting the right-wing forces, obtained only about 5,000 votes in Madrid, compared to the 224,000 votes received by Professor Besteiro, the leading Popular Front candidate. The Falange thus lost the two seats it had held in the preceding Cortes.

Dedicated principally to violent squadron activities – the "dialectic of fists and pistols," as José Antonio called them – the Falange had no specifically fascist characteristics, apart from symbol-bound imitations of its more powerful models: blue shirts, rather than black or brown ones; the yoke and arrows of the Catholic Kings rather than swastikas. Its leader, an individual of some depth and dedication to his cause, was an impassioned nationalist, nostalgic for the grandeur of Spain's remote past. Perhaps it was this conviction that made him regard his movement as absolutely subordinate to the

Created in the first half of the nineteenth century by the liberal-democratic government with the aim of controlling subversive movements in the countryside, the Guardia Civil were particularly hated by the peasant populace. They became central figures in many bloody repressions of strikes and land occupations.
© Publifoto

military order, to which he appealed a number of times for help in saving the country, even before the victory of the Popular Front.

And so the Falange played only an auxiliary role in the military's action at the moment of the coup. In the months preceding the coup – partly because of the martyr's halo bestowed on the party by its being outlawed, and by the arrest of José Antonio – the Falange attracted the Popular Front's bitterest enemies, especially younger people. But during the military rebellion, its actions were largely confined to doing the dirty work, the tasks of the so-called *limpieza*: cleaning up the back lines, hunting down and summarily eliminating all possible opponents of the "national movement."

Only later, as Franco consolidated his rule and sought to align himself with the Fascist powers, the Falange would rise to power as the only party. In doing so it would pay the price of further altering its original character.

JOSÉ ANTONIO PRIMO DE RIVERA

José Antonio Primo de Rivera, head of the Falange, was rather atypical compared to the other fascist leaders of his time. His support of fascism, rather than being ideological, seemed aimed at restoring Spain to the greatness of its past and at safeguarding the country from a socialist revolution. Even in classified documents, the Falange's subversive action is always presented as a preventive measure, a reaction against a "red" coup. In 1935, for example, in a report to the Italian embassy, from which he received periodical financial aid, he wrote: "If the socialist revolution breaks out against the government, the Falange, flanked by the Guardia Civil, may take over some villages, and perhaps a province, and proclaim national revolution." An alien to populist rhetoric, the leader of the Falange was in many ways a typical *señorito* – one of those young men from rich families who did not need to work, the sort capable of attracting the hatred of the masses. José Antonio did not reject the accusation of *señoritismo*, but contended that a *señorito* had, by definition, a responsibility to lead. This attitude emerges in the following passage of a speech made on the occasion of the founding of the Falange: "I would like this microphone in front of me to carry my voice into the furthest corners of the workers' homes, in order to say: yes, we wear ties; yes, you can say that we are *señoritos*. But we carry within us the will to fight for a goal that does not interest us as *señoritos*; we come to do battle so that many of those belonging to our class will be subjected to harsh and just sacrifices, and we come to do battle so that a totalitarian State will provide for the humble as well as the powerful. And we are this way because the *señoritos* of Spain have always been this way. That is how they succeeded in reaching the true ranks of gentlemen: in far-off lands and in our nation itself, they knew how to face death and take up the hardest missions, precisely for the sake of what was not in their interest, as *señoritos*." ■

(Primo de Rivera, J.A. *Obras*. Madrid, 1964. 62.)

Other Misfortunes of Democracy

The immediate aim of the authors of the military coup was to overthrow the country's government (which was the direct expression of a democratically-elected Parliament) and block the functions of its democratic institutions. But to what degree did the Republic represent democracy? How solid was this democracy? How much consensus could it boast, and how much of a tradition?

Son of the dictator, José Antonio Primo de Rivera (1906–1936) founded the Falange in 1933. In prison at the moment of the coup d'état – he had been condemned for the illicit detention of weapons – he was shot by the Republicans.

In December 1936, shortly after the successful defense of Madrid, the prime minister of the Republican government, Largo Caballero, received a warm letter from Stalin. In it the Soviet dictator (among other points) suggested that, unlike the Russian revolution, the Spanish revolution, now acting in resistance to the military rebellion, might follow the route of parliamentary democracy. This suggestion implied a request to reopen the Cortes (the Parliament), and restore its functions. Caballero, while thanking Stalin for his advice and aid, replied: "In answer to your suggestion, it is appropriate to point out that whatever opportunities the future holds in store for the parliamentary institution, it cannot boast enthusiastic supporters among us, even among Republicans."

That answer must certainly not have satisfied Stalin who, independently of the immediate interests of the USSR, well understood how useful it might be to re-evaluate those institutions that the Communist movement then defined as "bourgeois democracy," in order to encourage the democratic powers to come to the defense of the Republic. Nevertheless, while taking due account of Caballero's maximalist tendencies (now they called him the "Spanish Lenin," though he had been a reformist in the past), the prime minister's answer had some logic to it.

Parliamentary democracy could not boast a long tradition in the country, in fact; it tended to be discredited. Except for brief intervals, it had never worked in Spain. During much of the nineteenth century, forces had come to power by *pronunciamiento* rather than by election.

Miguel Primo de Rivera and King Alfonso XIII of Bourbon. Having come to power with the approval of the sovereign, General Primo de Rivera set up a personal dictatorship initially characterized by an awkward imitation of Italian fascism. His capricious, authoritarian conduct ended up alienating many sectors of the army and the courts. Abandoned as well by much of public opinion, which had first greeted him as a rebuilder of the corrupt Spanish political system, Primo de Rivera was finally forced to resign upon explicit request by the sovereign.

Then, for approximately half a century, from 1875 to 1923, a fraudulent scheme was set up which maintained only the appearance of a liberal and democratic system (universal suffrage was introduced in 1890). With this scheme, government was alternately assigned to two parties, the liberal and the conservative. By means of electoral fraud, they could count on annulling any opposition from the Cortes.

Such a system, which involved authorities at every level, from the king to the highest judiciary and administrative ranks, appeared to be driven by a will to satisfy partisan appetites and ambitions, rather than national ones. Corrupt and corrupting, it marked the demotion of Spain to a third-level power, mortifying the patriotism of much of the populace, as well as the desire of many intellectuals for Europeanization and respectability – including the great thinkers and artists that the country continued to generate, such as Ortega y Gasset, Unamuno and Pío Baroja. It is therefore easy to see why the coup d'état by General Primo de Rivera, who put an end to that pseudo-representative regime, was devoid of particular violence. Much of public opinion, disgusted by corruption, had seen in him that "iron surgeon" invoked at the beginning of the century by the Aragonese intellectual, Joaquín Costa: the creator of a temporary dictatorship capable of regenerating public life.

Gifted only with good will, but incapable – indeed, intolerant of any political mediation – the general was obviously destined to disappoint such expectations. At any rate, the fact that even reasonable men had been capable of embracing such an extravagant idea as that of a "dictatorial road to democracy," suggests how great a degree of misunderstanding and distrust of democratic and parliamentary institutions the system had caused. In the two-year period of 1930–1931, first the dictatorship and then the monarchy, which had supported it, crumbled under the weight of the malaise characterizing an expanding society that lacked functioning political institutions. With the advent of the Republic, men such as Azaña and Jiménez de Asua, who had continued to believe in liberal-democratic institutions, were offered the chance to create them; but they found it difficult to persuade their fellow countrymen.

Manuel Azaña votes during elections of representatives in 1931. Once the king had gone into exile after the defeat of the monarchist parties in the administrative elections of April 1931, the Republic was immediately proclaimed, and a provisory government set up. In June of the same year, elections were held for the Cortes (parliament). They were won by the Republican-Socialist coalition led by Azaña and Largo Caballero.
© Publifoto

The Republic: An Opportunity Beset by Problems

The task to be performed was particularly difficult, because it was certainly not possible to put limitations on such an operation of political engineering. In order to be accepted, the system had to produce a solution to the country's main problems that would be acceptable to the majority of Spaniards. First of all came the agrarian question, upon which all of Spain's economic and social stability depended, since it was still basically an agricultural country. In the south-central region, vast stretches of land were in the hands of a few big landowners, while landless peasants lived in misery – and the agrarian problem was even more multi-faceted and complex than what might be suggested by this fact alone. Every region was dramatically different from the next, so Spain required reforms capable of taking into account a variety of situations. Realistically, measures taken regarding different landowners would have to be varied in accordance with their political and social importance.

The Republic was proclaimed on April 14, 1931 after the administrative elections had proved how unpopular the sovereign was. During its first two years it was governed by a coalition of Republicans and Socialists, whose leaders were Manuel Azaña, the head of the government, and Largo Caballero, the Minister of Labor. Under pressure from a mass movement that agitated for social justice, the government's agrarian policy was led by doctrinal and maximalistic criteria, which ended up alienating from the Republic even those groups linked to small and medium-sized farm ownership.

The four generals,
Mother,
who rebelled
will be hanged
by Christmas Eve.
Madrid, how well you
resist
the bombers!
Laugh at the bombs
Madrileños.
– Republican song

To begin with, the agrarian reform of September 1932, in attempting to achieve a fairer and more productive distribution of land ownership, expropriated all property from absentee landowners, whatever the extent of their lands, whether they were uncultivated or rented out. Suddenly, the major landowners, who were basically members of the ancient nobility, gained a great number of allies, since land ownership was widespread among the urban middle classes, whose incomes were supplemented by land rental. So vast were the interests touched by agrarian reforms in the north-central regions, where property was broken up into smaller pieces, that such reforms had to be stalled in that area of the country. This upset everyone: both the owners under siege and the landless peasants. At the same time, the alliance among landowners, including those who directly managed their farms, was also strengthened by a series of measures that forbade free farm labor contracts. Such measures blocked or reduced land rental fees and brought about a rise in salaries that the falling prices of agricultural products made all the more onerous for owners.

Nevertheless, these provisions were unable to satisfy a vast, indigenous peasant movement that was thirsting for justice. The 1929 recession (which created an unfavorable context for the Republic's attempts at reform) had brought about overpopulation in the countryside by blocking the traditional safety valves of emigration; indeed, many unemployed men returned from the cities to their rural lands of origin.

How was it possible, then, to advocate moderation when there were landowners who still dominated the countryside in feudal style, who controlled the government so tightly as to prevent the institution of a land register in over half the nation (thus preventing fair taxation), and who, even in the face of the people's hunger, tried to reduce arable lands in order to obtain more profits?

Such attitudes on the part of landowners exasperated those who sought reforms, and many grew impatient with the long waiting periods necessary to execute expropriations. In fact, administrators tried to get around obstacles by issuing decrees permitting the temporary occupation of land that often had already been expropriated *de facto* or by forcibly imposing the cultivation of lands. All the necessary elements were in place for a head-on collision in the countryside. Indeed, both the landowners and the peasant movement organizations seemed to try to outdo one another in their intransigence.

A wartime poster of the FAI (Spanish Anarchist Federation). An agricultural country characterized by an extremely disproportionate distribution of property, Spain had to face the desperate problem of agrarian reform. The number of interests at stake, combined with the urgency of the situation and the competing strategies of the anarchist and socialist agrarian organizations, made any resolution nearly impossible.

At this point we can observe another peculiarity in the history of contemporary Spain, another lag with respect to that world history into whose midst the civil war would cast the country. We have seen how fascism and communism clashed at the gates of Madrid. But what presence, what weight, did communism wield in prewar Spain? At the moment of the coup, the communists were still a small force within the context of the workers' movement; a force that, in the Cortes, boasted only 15 out of the 257 representatives who constituted the majority of the Popular Front. The obtuse dependence of the Spanish Communist Party (PCE) on the directives of the International, which even led it to greet the advent of the Republic with open hostility, relegated the PCE to a marginal role.

In fact, the truly revolutionary wing of the Spanish workers' movement had traditionally been constituted by the anarchist movement. Concentrated particularly in the factories of Catalunya and in the countryside of Andalusia, it had suffered harsh repression during the dictatorship of Primo de Rivera, but sprang back bigger and stronger than ever with the birth of the Republic. The Federación Anarquista Ibérica (FAI), the ideological vanguard of the mass labor union, Conferacion Nacional del Trabajo (CNT), refused any form of gradualism, and promoted revolutionary strikes and forms of insurrection. As early as January 1932, the Republican-Socialist government was forced to face the "propaganda of facts" – that is, the anarchist insurrections breaking out, mostly on a provincial level, across all of Spain.

The anarchist movement grew during the Republican period because of the harsh poverty of the masses and the inevitable disappointment of their impatient demands for liberation. Amid such poverty and disappointment, how could people not distrust the new institutional system? How could people help but distrust this new government, when in the past a pseudo-liberal-democratic system had been passed off as a true democracy? The governments with which Spain had provided its people had been the rich soil for the growth of an ideology like anarchism, which hinges on the refusal of a State that is conceived as a falsity and an instrument of repression.

The first Republican government, headed by Manuel Azaña, with Caballero as Minister of Labor, found itself facing an overwhelming number of issues: from agrarian reform to reform of the armed forces, from the concession of autonomy to Basques and Catalans to the modification of the Church's role in public life.
© Publifoto

The workers' and peasant movement did boast, however – even in Spain – a reformist current, which was constituted by the Socialist Party. After extinguishing its revolutionary ambitions in an aborted insurrectional strike in 1917, the party was flanked by a strong labor union, the UGT (Unión General de Trabajadores), and for some time had proceeded along a gradualist road, which had even led it to collaborate with the regime of Primo de Rivera, during which it had remained the only legal workers' organization.

After coming of age in the shadow of the dictatorship, from which it had learned to dissociate itself, the Socialist Party was the majority party in the first Republican Cortes: it represented the most radical wing of the government. In the countryside, its labor union grew considerably in the first two years of the Republic, partly because of the advantages its militants gained by government protection. Goaded by the anarchist labor union, however, it began to absorb the latter's tendency toward anti-ownership radicalism, thus giving up any mediating function capable of filtering and attenuating conflicts. In the countryside, hatred and violence began to foment civil war.

But it was not only these economic issues that stirred up the civil strife. Social conflicts were strained and made harsher because of the profound disagreement over the role of the Catholic Church in public life. What would otherwise have been a fairly simple episode of class conflict thus became quite complicated. With this issue in the mix, the landowners found ample support among the many faithful, who felt themselves to be dramatically threatened by a Republican policy they regarded as sacrilegious.

A leader of the Catholic Right, José María Gil Robles admired and often imitated the Fascist dictators. The great alarm this caused on the Left contributed to bringing events to a head the moment Gil Robles took office as War Minister in October 1938.

In order to understand that policy, which has been called the "inevitable error," we need to focus on certain traits that characterized the presence of the Church in Spanish society at the time. Deprived during the nineteenth century of much of its material power by the progressive expropriation of the immense lands in its possession, the Church had nevertheless succeeded in relaunching its political influence (if on a reduced, eighteenth-century scale) and permeating society. As Spain faced an increase in social insubordination, a decline in international stature, and the birth of regional nationalisms – Catalan, Basque, Galician – the Church offered the dominant classes an instrument for pacifying and uniting the masses: Catholic nationalism. In linking Catholicism with the glory of Spain's past, this ideology compensated for the country's frustration and decadence. But the church showed a different side, too, as it provided many of the basic social services – schools, health structures, assistance – the poor and absentee government could not manage. Of course, this succeeded in revitalizing the presence of the Church, especially amid the lower and middle classes.

At the same time, the Church's expansion was paralleled by the growth of anticlericalism. Not only a bourgeois anticlericalism of intellectual origin, but most strik-

THE CHURCH AND SOCIETY

At the moment when the Republic came to power, the influence of the Church in Spanish society had spread far beyond religious rites and the consciences of the faithful. A great number of social services were entrusted to it: numerous hospitals, mental institutions, homes for the elderly, orphanages, reformatories, and soup kitchens for the poor were directly managed by religious communities and ecclesiastical orders. And in almost all the other publicly-administrated ones, the presence of religious Catholics among the staff was considerable. In such institutions, the people assisted were often obliged to maintain a type of conduct and practice suitable to that of a religious novice – replete with masses, prayers and hymns throughout the day. Many lay persons who needed the help of these institutions resented the religion that was pushed on them. And it was in the realm of education especially that the church had substituted the state in its tasks. According to official statistics, about 20 percent of elementary school students attended religious institutions – often without paying; unofficially, the number was much higher, because many towns and provinces, who were legally responsible for providing primary instruction, assigned the task to religious centers. An even greater percentage of secondary school students attended religious schools, although there are no precise statistics. These schools tended to offer a much more serious curriculum than public ones. Many sons of the bourgeoisie, even those who were lukewarm toward the church, attended Jesuit and Scolopian schools. If we consider how vast the Church's presence was in the realm of education, the new constitutional rule forbidding it to teach seems foolish, and even harmful to the freedom of education. Such a change required an enormous effort – and indeed, such an effort was made – to secularize teaching entirely, in an extremely short period of time.

But if we consider the contents of the instruction given by the church, we can understand how urgent it was for the state to restore its educative function as much as possible. In 1934, for example, in a textbook widely adopted in Catholic girls' high schools, one could read the following passage regarding freedom of opinion: "The filthy sewer, the hungry savage beast, the insatiable and bloody freedom to err which has been generated by the law of majority power, is the savage law of the strongest, the seed of ruin and death." ■

ingly, a popular anticlericalism that sometimes broke out in bloody episodes, in the burning of churches and convents. It struck not only urban centers, but also the countryside, where it often coexisted, and more or less openly clashed, with the most fervid Catholicism.

This popular anticlericalism, which led Catholics to speak with bitter wonder of "mass apostasy," coexisted with the growing influence of anarchism in a circular relationship of cause and effect. More than feeding on ideology, it was nurtured by men's sense of having been cheated and betrayed by a Church that refused to recognize the basic rights of citizens, and that time and again supported the dominant classes against the claims of the people. Even the Church's provision of social services, rather than inspiring support, often gave rise to bitter protest, since these services were dispensed as "charity" and receiving them required the observance of moral precepts and fulfillment of ritualistic practices: going to mass, reciting prayers, and so on.

Although the Church's attitude at the moment of passage from monarchy to Republic was at first one of prudent waiting, its traditional ideological position, as manifested from the pulpit, its teachings, and its press, was not long in clashing with the new authorities and the new institutions. In particular, the Republic's plan for secularizing the state was destined to come up against the harshest resistance on the part of Catholics. And the conflict would quickly reach the boiling point, since the necessary secularization measures would be accompanied by punitive provisions smacking of a vengeance that mortified religious sentiment.

As early as the fall of 1931, after a fierce debate in the Cortes, the approval of Article 26 of the Constitution immediately rendered church-state relations openly hostile. According to that article, the Catholic Church, which until then had been the official state religion, protected and favored by the monarchy, was reduced to the rank of any other "association," deprived of any public financial support, prevented from "exercising industry, commerce and teaching," and made subject to the unconditional expropriation of its property. That same article also annulled the Jesuit Order and nationalized its patrimony.

Left, Alfonso XIII visiting the Convent of the Calatravas (Cadavers), in 1911.
Above, a violently anticlerical poster, which was widely displayed in the Republican zone during the war. The traditional alliance between throne and altar seriously harmed the Church's position, once the Republic came to power. And when the Azaña government attempted to secularize the country, the Church responded with equal intransigence, clearly siding with the Right.

In August 1932, slightly less than a year after the proclamation of the Republic, the pronunciamiento in Seville by General Sanjurjo (to the right) was the first attempt at a military coup. Four years after that failed attempt, Sanjurjo was designated by the conspiring military as the future Head of State, once the Popular Front government was abolished. But an airplane crash prevented him from ever taking office.
Below, a demonstration in support of President Zamora.
© 2 Publifoto

The new constitutional norms were really quite extreme: for one thing, forbidding teaching created immediate problems for the state, since most of the country's schools were Catholic. But Catholics felt even more threatened and mortified by successive laws regarding religious faiths and congregations, particularly because local authorities often exploited this law in order to dominate and molest. For example, the need for permits from public authorities in order to celebrate public ceremonies outside religious buildings, often resulted in prohibiting traditional processions and open-air masses. The symbols of worship – crucifixes, sacred images and so forth – were removed from schools, public buildings, streets and squares, though the faithful who wished to continue to display such symbols were, of course, still subject to taxation. Moreover, local

Republican authorities tried to encourage civil marriages and funerals and secularize cemeteries, thus further wounding the sensitivities and convictions of a Catholic populace that already felt under siege.

The Catholics and the landowners, who were often the same people, found support in the CEDA (Confederación de Derechas Autónomas), a party led by a brilliant lawyer, José María Gil Robles. This right-wing party was the legal opposition to the Republican-Socialist government; the aborted *pronunciamiento* by General

Sanjurjo in August of 1932 was the illegal opposition. But the proto-fascist style of its charismatic leader, Gil Robles, the great assemblies where his followers gathered, and the paramilitary formation of his youth organization awakened deep fear for the survival of the liberal-democratic system.

Meanwhile, the government coalition was falling apart, squeezed between two extreme opposition movements. Social conditions were explosive; unemployment had increased enormously. In Estremadura and in Andalusia people went on strike, broke machinery, and stole crops. In many places, peasants, impatient over the slow application of the reforms, occupied land. In Barcelona, in Biscay, and in the mines of Asturias, men went on strike to protest the firings and the reduction of salaries. In January 1933 the CNT once more headed a revolt, which spread quickly, particularly in the west and in Andalusia. It was in the Andalusian village, Casas Viejas, that the police carried out a horrible massacre, for which the government was blamed. The socialists, under pressure from their own grassroots ranks and from their anarchist competition, assumed more and more radical attitudes and began to dissociate themselves from the government coalition, which was thrown into a crisis by dissidence from many Republicans as well.

Defeated in the election for Supreme Court members, the government resigned, and since there was no majority in support of a new government, new elections were called. The parties of the old coalition presented a fractured front to the voters, the anarchists called for abstention and, since the majority electoral system favored blocs, the center-right alliance, which was made up of Alejandro Lerroux's radical party and that of Gil Robles, obtained the relative majority of seats.

Thus the reformist experience of the first two years of the Republic came to an end. It deserved credit for having made a great effort at democratic renewal – besides creating the progressive Constitution and enacting agrarian reforms, it had issued a statute for the autonomy of Catalunya, reformed the armed forces, and set up a vast program of public instruction. But it had

A leader of the Catalan Left Republican Party (ERC), Luis Companys held office as president of the Catalan government during the October 1934 insurrection, which attempted to gain the independence Catalunya. Companys was imprisoned after the failure of this attempt, but following the victory of the Popular Front, he once again occupied his former post, which he held for the duration of the civil war.
© Sergi i Octavi Centelles

failed to find a coherent line of conduct with the exasperated masses – now they were repressed, now mollified, but more by symbolic gestures than by substantial concessions of their rights.

1934: The Year of the Great Fear

1934 is a crucial year for understanding the civil war that would soon follow. Thick with events, it was dominated by fear. Fear grew, ricocheted against those who generated it, and bounced back against the adversary, in a long tennis match that lasted until July 1936.

The first cause for fear was the ominous shadow cast by international events: in January of 1933, Hitler had come to power in Germany by election; in February 1934, the Austrian Chancellor, Dollfuss, who had set up a sort of clerico-fascist regime, squashed the socialist movement in a bloody repression. Dollfuss's image was projected onto that of Gil Robles, who, for his part, often imitated the attitudes and conduct of the Fascist dictators: in the plazas his followers greeted him to the cry of "*Jefe, jefe!*" – the Spanish version of "*Duce, duce!*" – and in the Cortes, he declared more than once that if the Right did not achieve its aims by parliamentary means, it would do so without the Parliament; and he proclaimed his intention of eradicating all revolutionary movements. But who was afraid of whom? Even before the Azaña government fell, Caballero had been proclaiming his intention to transform Spain into a Socialist Republic; and as far as methods were concerned, he also was not about to limit himself to democratic and parliamentary means.

But practically speaking, Gil Robles followed a very gradual line of conduct. Though he had majority support, he maintained an appearance of loyalty to the Lerroux government (which, contrary to fears, did not hasten to dismantle the reforms of the preceding two years). Nevertheless, as early as December 1933, the anarchists carried out an insurrection. As always, it was sporadic and uncoordinated; as always, it was put down. Perhaps more significantly, the Socialist Party, convinced of the need for preventive action, prepared its own insurrection. Gil Robles inspired such fear that not only Caballero, but also the more moderate wing of the party, collaborated with the revolutionary plans, and even a reformist leader like Indalecio Prieto organized traffic in weapons.

As social struggles became more bitter (in particular, a farm workers' strike in the summer of 1934 affected all of Spain), the government exasperated the opposition by giving amnesty to the military leaders of the 1932 coup and blocking enactment of the reforms. A conflict broke out between the central government and the regional government of Catalunya over a law passed by the latter that favored the access of peasants to land ownership. The Supreme Court proclaimed the incompetence of the Catalan government, thereby exacerbating the autonomy problem. The monarchic-militarist Right, a fierce adversary of regional autonomy, rejoiced: "I prefer a red Spain to a broken Spain," claimed its leader, Calvo Sotelo.

In this climate, Gil Robles intentionally provoked his adversaries by calling for the CEDA to have a role in the government. That signal drove the Socialist Party to set off a preventive revolution meant to block the "resistible ascent" of Gil Robles. The action was ill-planned; the moment was the one chosen by the adversary; but when on October 4, Lerroux began to reorganize the government, entrusting three ministries to the CEDA, the action was taken up just the same. A general strike was proclaimed, the most important cities blocked; but the countryside, weakened by the long summer strike, did not follow suit. In Madrid, during a four-day period, in some working-class neighborhoods barricades were raised; socialist militias assaulted the Ministry of the Interior, the police parking lot, and the central post office, clashing repeatedly with the police forces. But in the rest of the country, armed

A moderate reformer and State advisor during the dictatorship of Primo de Rivera, Largo Caballero progressively radicalized his opinions after the first two years of Republican government, so much as to be nicknamed the "Spanish Lenin." In October 1934 he was among the promotors of the insurrection opposing the CEDA's entry into government, and consequently was imprisoned.
© Publifoto

Forces faithful to the government patrol the Plaça Catalunya in Barcelona. The 1934 uprisings ended in failure, both in Madrid and Barcelona, where the military garrison commanded by General Batet successfully opposed the proclamation of independence without finding much resistance.
© Sergi i Octavi Centelles

conflict was rare and of short duration. The revolution in the capital, too, was soon put down. The revolutionary committee, along with all the main Socialist leaders – including Caballero – were arrested.

The revolution succeeded only in Asturias. Led by unified organizations (the *Alianzas Obreras*) composed of socialists, anarchists and communists, it spread out from the mineral basin toward the provincial capital, Oviedo. That city surrendered after a few days of fighting in the streets. During the next few days the region was controlled by the revolutionaries, headed by a committee in charge of all governing functions. The government troops converging on Oviedo from Castile and from Galicia were blocked by worker militias. In this phase, what would later be exalted by the workers' movement as the "October Revolution in Asturias" had not yet become particularly bloody. Of course there were casualties, some summary executions – especially of members of the hated Guardia Civil; and as a sinister presage of the civil war which would follow, massacres of Catholics. But when the revolutionary troops finally had to surrender to the African legionary army that had landed at Gijon, the repression was fierce: more than 1,000 died, many immediately executed by shooting; 30,000 were taken prisoner, and many of these tortured. The repression was led by Franco, Yagüe, and Varela: all future protagonists of the military revolt.

Catalunya rebelled at the same time Asturias did. The regional government, another victim of the great fear of Gil Robles, feared the imminent abrogation of its autonomy, and so declared the independence of Catalunya. This action was absolutely foolhardy in its ambition, since it was not even supported by the workers' movement. The revolt was destined to be repressed within a few hours by an army that was particularly averse to separatism.

At the end of October, a long line of prisoners, including Largo Caballero, the Catalan president Louis Companys, and even Manuel Azaña, gave the image of a nation yoked to the victorious cart of the Right.

After failing in all the rest of the country, the 1934 revolt was kept alive for two weeks in the mineral basin of Asturias, where the rebels won out over the local authorities, and were defeated only after elite Legion troops were sent. Operations were coordinated by Franco (here with the commander of the Guardia Civil, Doval) and carried out on the battlefield by General Lopez Ochoa.

Toward Civil War

After the revolt of July 1936, the military attempted to justify their actions by claiming that they had needed to prevent the Communist coup d'état that was in the making. This accusation was totally unfounded and even a bit ridiculous, given the extremely limited influence of the Communist Party. But if what they really meant was that there was an imminent revolutionary threat, then their claims were not devoid of credibility, since the recent past had shown more than one sign pointing in that direction. Indeed, one must consider what 1934 had meant, and what had followed when contemplating why so many had given the coup such solid support. That year a huge revolt had been attempted, and had temporarily succeeded in more than one region. The revolt had intended not only to prevent a change in the makeup of a national gov-

ernment, which was absolutely normal and legitimate in the context of a liberal-democratic system, but actually to set up a Socialist Republic.

This action was certainly inspired by the "Great Fear": that is, the fear of seeing Spain repeat recent experiences in Germany. Germany's example seemed to confirm the conviction that only a socialist revolution could stop fascism. But that conviction had in turn induced its opposite on the other side: that is, the conviction that only a reactionary coup d'état could prevent the liberal-democratic system from degenerating into a revolutionary regime. All in all, very few people in Spain actually believed in the value and stability of the democratic Republic.

***A** column of prisoners after the Asturias revolt. A harsh repression followed the defeat of the rebels, with many summary executions and long prison sentences. Throughout Spain, the repression also struck a great number of workers who, though not directly involved in the events, paid with the loss of their jobs. The Spanish Popular Front was born of the desire to give back freedom and jobs to all those who had lost them after the incidents of October 1934.*

© L'Illustration/Sygma T

Nonetheless, the "Great Fear" turned out to be unjustified, at least in the short term. After the events of October, the Left was essentially at the mercy of the Right. No time could have been better for Gil Robles to attempt a takeover. But nothing of the sort happened. Instead, the repression was extremely harsh: several death sentences were given (though many others were commuted), and thousands were sentenced to long terms in prison. Even more lost their jobs; hundreds of local administrations were dissolved. The reforms of the preceding period were blocked and sabotaged; the agrarian reform was distorted; permits for the temporary occupation of lands were not renewed; the statute for the autonomy of Catalunya was suspended. This was the darkest moment of a period that the Left would call the "*bienio negro*." But Gil Robles succeeded only in gaining the War Ministry (in which office he appointed Franco Head of State); and the nation continued to be led by a center-right coalition that governed within the limits of the Constitution, though it was preparing a revision of that document.

In this climate, which was respectful enough toward

constitutional liberties, the Left was able to re-emerge and unite in a Popular Front pact. A crisis of the government coalition, which was weakened by several episodes of corruption, provided the right chance. The president of the Republic, the Catholic Alcalá Zamora, refused to assign the power to form a new government to Gil Robles, who in turn failed to gain the military support necessary for the coup he was planning, but at the same time opposed any other solution. Thus new elections were held, which facilitated the birth of a left-wing coalition galvanized by the determination to eliminate the effects of the post-October repression. This determination was widely shared by the anarchists. The coalition demanded the liberation of prisoners and the re-hiring of

Barcelona celebrates the victory of the Popular Front in 1936. Thanks to the majority electoral law, the Popular Front managed to gain a considerable majority of seats in the Cortes even though the two coalitions had received nearly the same number of votes.
© Sergi i Octavi Centelles

ELECTIONS OF FEBRUARY 1936

The rival forces in the elections of February 1936 were the Popular Front, which was composed of sixteen parties (the most important of which were the Socialist Party, Manuel Azaña's Left Republican Party and Diego Martínez Barrio's Unión Republicana); the rightist bloc, concentrating mostly around the CEDA; and a center coalition inspired by the president of the Republic.
Of 13,553,710 potential voters, 72 percent cast their ballot and, according to the most reliable estimate, the Popular Front gained 48 percent of the vote, the rightist bloc 46 percent, and the center group, including the Basque nationalists, 5–6 percent. Though the election was extremely close, the technicalities of the electoral law allowed the Popular Front to gain 263 (55 percent) of the 473 seats in the Cortes, which allowed it to govern with a wide majority margin. An analysis of the vote highlights the success of the Front in the big cities, and strong support for the Right in the countryside of Castile. ■

The prisoners taken in 1934 leave jail. The victory of the Popular Front was cheered throughout Spain, in demonstrations accompanied by the immediate liberation of prisoners of the "October Revolution."
© L'Illustration/Sygma/T

those who had lost their jobs. The birth of the Popular Front helped create two distinct opposing poles, by inspiring the creation of a right-wing alliance that excluded the parties of the center.

The election results revealed a country broken up into two blocs, with each bloc having a nearly equal number of votes. But the electoral law sent the Popular Front to power, converting the meager majorities obtained in the election into conspicuous majorities. This situation was exacerbated by the winners' thirst for revenge, and the losers' fear of revolution. Just a few hours after the polls were closed, the signs pointing to future events appeared: while crowds liberated prisoners even before the electoral results were complete, many military men put pressure on the president of the Republic in favor of a coup.

Under pressure from the masses, the Popular Front government, headed by Azaña, set out to annul all the effects of the *bienio negro*. The prisoners taken in October were given amnesty, those who had been fired regained their jobs, and "red" administrators were reinstated. The agrarian reform started up again and began to be enacted more rapidly; imposed cultivation of the

LARGO CABALLERO AND THE THREAT OF REVOLUTION

After being State advisor to the dictator, Primo de Rivera, Francisco Largo Caballero began to radicalize his policies more and more. In this, he was influenced by several young Marxist intellectuals – such as Luis Araquistaín and Julio Alvárez del Vayo – who congregated around the journal, *Leviatán*; but he was also driven by the need to oppose the other outstanding figure of the Socialist Party, the reformist, Indalecio Prieto. Without a doubt, especially after October 1934, his opinions began to awaken great apprehension among moderates. For example, on the eve of the elections in February 1936, he affirmed: "The bourgeois class and its representatives think that in our country we have already reached the goal of political institutions, and we must tell them we have not. The Republic is not immutable. The bourgeois Republic is not incapable of change. The bourgeois Republic is not an institution that we must consolidate so as to make achievement of our goals impossible. How must we achieve them? In every way possible! We have already said so a thousand times. Our objective is to conquer political power. The method? Any method we are able to use!" ■

land increased – whether by decree or autonomous action on the part of the labor unions. The autonomy of Catalunya was restored, and voting was under way to decide the fate of Basque independence.

As less and less room was left for moderation, fears grew. The moderate Alcalá Zamora – who had managed to defend democracy at decisive moments – was removed from the presidency on a pretext, and replaced with Azaña. The Socialists would not allow their reformist leader, Prieto, to form the new government (that task was entrusted to the Galician autonomist, Casares), and instead resumed revolutionary talk, while strengthening their ties to the Communist Party. The Right, already feeling the blows against its interests and frightened by further threats, made preparations for a counter-revolution. The military actively conspired. The Falange, joined by new militants, committed a number of terrorist attacks and was outlawed, while José Antonio was sentenced to several months in prison for the illegal detention of weapons.

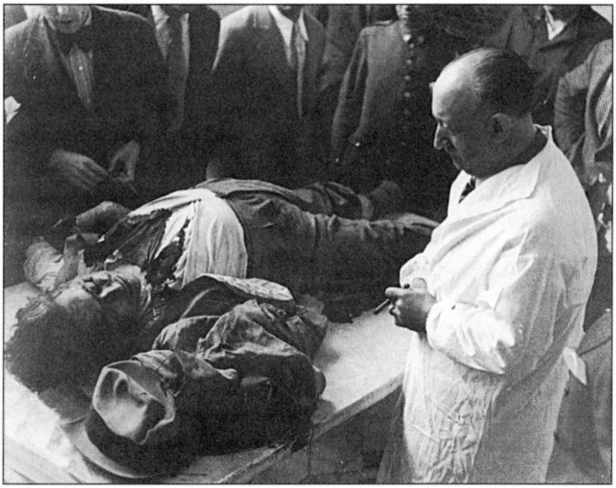

An advocate of the monarchist right, Calvo Sotelo was assassinated in reprisal for the terrorist attack in which Lieutenant José del Castillo, who sympathized with the Left, was killed. The fact was all the more serious in that Calvo Sotelo was virtually the head of parliamentary opposition.

The Left was no less violent. In mid-June, Gil Robles denounced before the Cortes 269 homicides in four months, 170 burnings of churches, and 133 general strikes, carried out in particular by the anarchists of the CNT. Those figures were exaggerated, but they did reflect the disastrous situation of public law and order. When this spiral of violence reached Calvo Sotelo, the leader of the parliamentary opposition to the Republic – he was forced out of his house and killed in cold blood – it was no longer possible to deny that the fragile Spanish democracy was in serious trouble. When summer came, the country was falling headlong into civil war.

Chapter 3

FROM COUP D'ÉTAT TO REVOLUTION

THE FAILED COUP SPARKS OFF A REVOLUTIONARY PROCESS THAT THE GOVERNMENT SUCCEEDS IN CONTROLLING ONLY IN PART. STILL, IN THE FACE OF HIGH HOPES FOR SOCIAL REDEMPTION, THE REVOLUTION HIGHLIGHTS THE DEEP GAPS DIVIDING THE REPUBLICANS.

Despite what the supporters of Franco's regime had been claiming for decades, no revolution – whether Communist, Socialist or libertarian – was in the making in Spain between the spring and summer of 1936. Social conflict and violent clashes remained primarily in the countryside. Except for Madrid, the cities were rather tranquil. In the main industrial centers of the nation, without whose involvement any revolutionary action would have been inconceivable, no particularly harsh conflict was registered. Barcelona, the industrial capital, was even spoken of as an "oasis of peace."

In Barcelona, where the anarchists bore the brunt of the struggle against the rebels at the time of the coup, a genuine revolution broke out. On the front of this double-decker bus, a sign of the CNT, the anarchist labor union, marks the collectivization of city transport. The collectivization of all activities, from the means of production to the consumer goods of everyday life, became the anarchists' central goal.
© Sergi i Octavi Centelles

Revolution Spreads

Ironically, it was actually the failed coup itself that seemed to start a revolutionary process in the cities and countryside. Not only as an inevitable reaction to the aborted attack, but because in the face of the liberal-democratic government's incapacity to prevent and put down the coup d'état, more radical forces could easily present themselves as the only barrier against militarism and fascism. After all, it had actually been the popular forces, led by anarchist and socialist organizations, who had waged armed battle in the streets and squares, beating the military supporters of the coup.

The winners wanted to pick the fruit of their victory immediately. Everywhere, they created governing bodies that not only replaced the old local administrations, but also took on tasks of wider scope, such as the orga-

During the war, even the most remote towns of Republican Spain expressed their independence from the central government, and they printed the money to show it; see examples of the banknotes issued by the Villarrobledo Muncipal Council and the Papiol Junta. As many as 10,000 different monies have been counted, including coins and bills, printed by about 2,000 different bodies, half of which were Catalan.

nization of militias to fight against the coup forces for control of the territory, the administration of justice, and the control of production. The scenario in Republican Spain following the July battles reflected a widespread will among those who had opposed the military to continue the battle by carrying out a full-fledged revolution; but this desire was dispersed and fractured into small, contradictory movements. It was not quite a twentieth-century revolution, but instead carried forward the nineteenth-century tradition of the local sovereign. Like the *alcalde* of Móstoles who had declared war on Napoleon, the *juntas* of the provincial areas assumed self-government of the cities, and then behaved toward other cities as sovereign authorities, every time there was a *pronunciamiento* or insurrection.

In the Spain of 1936 things were not much different. Valencia saw the creation of a Comité Ejecutivo Popular, formed by parties of the Popular Front and the CNT, which took over all governing powers. Similar bodies emerged: in Malaga, with the glorious name of Comité de Salud Publica; in Asturias, where the bellicose Comité de Guerra of Gijón was countered by the more modest Comité Provincial of Oviedo; in the Basque country, and in Santander. Not only the big cities and the provincial capitals were swept up in this phenomenon; indeed, all of the Republican area, from Castile to western Andalusia, was scattered with small independent and sovereign committees. And any traveler who had to drive from Madrid to Valencia was forced to stop at no fewer than twenty road blocks in order to have his documents checked by each local committee.

A revolutionary process should rapidly grow through such a phase and pass beyond it, in order to allow a new centralization of power. Yet that did not happen. The Giral government limited itself to legalizing the situation, by recognizing the new authorities *de facto*. But the *gobernadores civiles*, the prefects who before the war had dominated the provinces at will, remained little more than decorative figureheads, while no political force attempted to spearhead any of the revolutionary movements so that they could find expression in local government.

The responsibility for this gap between the center and the margins, a gap that would come to seriously harm the Republican front, was, politically speaking, the anarchist movement's. The anti-state ideology expressed by the anarchists prevented or slowed any efficient solution, whether it be the creation of a central revolutionary government, or – as the other side wished – the restoration of the old forms of government. But we must emphasize that the anarchist movement was, for its part, an expression of widespread localism. The wave of "*consejismo*" (the tendency to create councils and committees) that was washing over Republican Spain, and the successive reluctance to cede power, saw not only the anarchists as protagonists at the local level, but also socialists, Republicans and a great number of individuals who had, at least initially, no party. And so the problem was never solved, even when the leaders of the CNT and the FAI came to the point of making the great compromise of joining the Republican government (an absolutely unprecedented event in the history of international anarchism).

Republican militiamen control traffic from a bridge in the Republican zone. The fracturing of power immediately after the failed coup was one of the characteristic traits of Republican Spain, as shown by the many checkpoints set up by widely varied independent and sovereign committees.
© Publifoto

As early as September the Giral government, which was now verifiably incapable of confronting the new situation, had ceded power to a government headed by Largo Caballero, in which all of the Popular Front parties were represented. In early November, in the face of the threat looming over Madrid, Largo Caballero was able to bring four anarchist ministers into the government. The leaders of the CNT and the FAI gave in to being "blackmailed" by the need for unity and solidarity, at this most dangerous moment of antifascist resistance. Caballero hoped that such cohesion would make governing the country easier. But he was soon to be disappointed.

The union of war and revolution would always lie at the base of the anarchists' philosophy, as shown in this FAI poster. Despite their ambition to closely link collectivized production to the necessity for war (the chimney turns into a cannon), Catalunya would never be able to supply the front through its war industry.

For a long time, even to this day, the anarchist movement has had a great debate over whether or not the anarchists' participation in the government in fact jeopardized a possible revolutionary victory in the civil war. But such an argument has no basis in fact. To begin with, their participation did not suffocate any burgeoning body of revolutionary government. And such participation did not substantially change anything in the relationship between the government and local powers, except in terms of the war effort. A centralized, regular army began to form (but not without a great deal of resistance, and not always with success). The fact is, with the exception of military operations and foreign policy, the Caballero government did not fully administer a single thing. In reality, short of having coordinating bodies that the anarchists themselves would have controlled, the situation had more in common with a confederation of free communes as imagined by the anarchists, than with a government having authority over the entire Republican territory.

A View of Barcelona and the Countryside

No place was better than the Catalan capital for grasping the dynamics of revolutionary events. There, street fighting against the rebel military forces was sustained mainly by the anarchists. And the victory was theirs. The president of Catalunya, Companys, openly acknowledged this fact by offering them power, in a clever move that unmasked their inability to exercise it. The men of the CNT were evasive; they left Companys at his post of command, and joined together with the Popular Front in forming a committee of antifascist militias; then they joined the restored autonomous government of Catalunya.

That error was less significant than may appear. As things went, the city was virtually in the hands of the anarchists, and they could now dedicate themselves to the "constructive work" of revolution. Barcelona offered everyone who came – antifascist volunteers, revolutionaries, correspondents, adventurers – an extraordinarily exciting spectacle. The elegant, avant-garde city, with its *barrio chino* and its crowded, colorful Ramblas, had become the background for a new revolutionary show. Everywhere one could see bourgeois clothing replaced with the uniforms of workers and militias, the red and black neckerchiefs of anarchy, the restaurants converted into public canteens, the expropriated shops declaring their new, collective ownership. The anarchists' strength could be felt above all in the economic changes being made. In October, they managed to get the autonomous government to issue an act collectivizing industries that had more than 100 employees, as well as industries that had been abandoned by their owners. And in practice, the labor union committees had the power of imposing this decree even beyond its legal limits.

But what exactly did collectivization mean? In their debates, the anarchists had actually given precedence to the need for "socialization," by which they meant that the productive activities of each single enterprise should benefit the whole of society. But in practice, the same problem that afflicted the central government in its relations with the local powers on the political level, reappeared on the economic level. What body had enough power to make a change like

Besides public services – trams, water, gas, electricity – and food markets, collectivization in Catalunya also reached retail sales. This poster by a collective in Barcelona announces a "white sale" with big discounts.

collectivization last? The economic planning boards in the Catalan government had difficulty imposing their directives on the collectivized enterprises; the latter were more preoccupied with production and salaries than with marketing, while the managing committees, mostly of union origin, were mainly interested in the well-being of the factory workers (at best) or of committee members (at worst). How could these conflicting interests be reconciled with the centralization effort necessary to create a war industry?

Leaving Barcelona, one went on to face the Aragon front. The first foreign volunteers – those from France – hastened there. And they were joined by others. Carlo Rosselli, who fought with an Italian contingent, was among the first to live through the experience. He left a written report which, though passionate, betrayed his perplexity. He recorded the great enthusiasm among the militia and the people in the towns through which the volunteers passed. But then combat slowed; during the entire war, Franco was never again seriously engaged in

REVOLUTIONARY BARCELONA

Especially in the first months of war, Barcelona was the desired destination for revolutionaries from all over the world. One of these, the German, H.E. Kaminski, thus describes the city in those extraordinary days: "On the Ramblas, at every hour of the day and night, an enormous crowd pushes onto the central avenue, while street vendors sell flowers and birds. One could call it a permanent fair. Many men and some women are now wearing militia uniforms. They are often armed with rifles, and it is not unusual to see a militia soldier shouldering his weapon, walking arm-in-arm with his wife, holding his child's hand. The cars, which make a great deal of noise, are no longer private vehicles. They all bear signs indicating political organizations, or the insignia of the authorities, and they always carry a flag, usually a huge one...

"On the Ramblas and on the other main streets, all the buildings capable of becoming administrative centers have been occupied. The Communists have settled into the Hotel Colón, and the anarchists have taken over the house of the factory owners' syndicate. In all the shops there is a sign hung up indicating the new form of management. In front of banks and political offices, armed sentinels stand guard... No one must be hungry in the new Barcelona. The gastronomic union feeds all the needy at noon and in the evening. To be admitted, at first you need authorization from an organization or committee, but no bureaucratic practices are adopted. Those presenting no document are fed, too. These meals are distributed in numerous hotels and restaurants, including the Ritz. While waiting their turn, the poor line up in the streets." ■

– Kaminski, H.E. *Ceux de Barcelone*; Italian translation *Quelli di Barcellona*. Milan: Il Saggiatore, 1966. 24–30.

that region. On one side the central government and Popular Front accused the Catalan government and the anarchists of cowardice and empty boasting. For their part, the anarchists denounced the losses on the Aragon front, where the necessary weapons had not been sent, because of jealousy and political squabbling. Catalunya, the only area of Republican Spain to have sufficiently developed industry to set up a war machine capable of supplying the nearby front, would fail to do so. Also, the anarchists put up a long resistance to the militarization of the militia, preferring to maintain the organization essentially as it was: that is, militias that were rich with enthusiasm, but not very efficient.

Furthermore, in Aragon, too, the anarchists' main concern was to achieve a revolution. Here, as elsewhere, this meant collectivization, above all. But unlike that of Barcelona, collectivization was radical here. Nor was it limited to the means of production (especially land): it spread to consumer goods as well. The whole economy was controlled by local committees, which

An anarchist militiaman leaving for the Aragon front. The improvised, politicized militias, which were sustained by an enthusiasm that the Republic had tried to tap in order to make up for its lack of a reliable, well-trained army, were progressively militarized through reintegration of the most trustworthy officers, and the formation of new commanding echelons of popular origin. This reorganization aroused considerable resistance, above all among the anarchists.
© Sergi i Octavi Centelles

A poster by the UGT, the socialist trade union, exhorts peasants to contribute to the war effort. Left unresolved by the Agrarian Reform of 1932, the agrarian question came to the fore again in wartime. Collectivization of the land spread throughout Republican Spain, though not without opposition and violence.

made decisions on tasks and workloads, on the distribution of products "according to need" (in many towns, money was abolished), and on the provision of services. Adherence to the collectives was voluntary, but was certainly influenced by the presence of armed militia columns, including the one led by the legendary libertarian commandant, Buenaventura Durruti. Tasks involving the orientation and coordination, exchange and commercialization of products, in an economy having a dangerous tendency to self-consumption, were carried out by the Aragon Council, which was controlled by the anarchists, but included members of the Popular Front, and was also recognized by the central government.

Enthusiastic witnesses have left us an image of laborious, prosperous communes formed voluntarily and directed by democratically-elected bodies. Their adversaries, though, spoke of peasants subjected to the tyranny of the committees or militia columns who lived off their produce and threatened them with violence if they did not comply with the local committee's wishes. It is difficult to untangle these contrasting accounts because in both cases, we have what would seem reliable testimony. Without a doubt, Aragon, unlike much of Spain, was a territory of many small landowners, who were probably reluctant to comply with mass collectivization. On the other hand, it is true that after August 1937, when the Aragon collectives were dissolved by the central government with the help of the army, many of them were gradually reconstituted.

Nevertheless, the collectivization phenomenon was not an exclusively Catalan-Aragonese one. Certainly, in no city of Republican Spain did collectivization reach the intensity it did in Barcelona (partly because no other city enjoyed the same level of industrialization); and in many cases, the collective enterprise was instituted only in factories and shops abandoned by their proprietors. But

Right, a division of the popular militia engaged in the Sierra during the battle for Madrid.
© Publifoto

it was different in the countryside: from Cordoba to Jaén, from Ciudad Real to Cuenca, to the Valencian *huerta*, collectivization was widespread. It could not have been any different: this change had been fought for by the most important peasant organizations, not only by the anarchists, but also by the Socialist labor union. Nonetheless, as in other areas, it did not proceed without episodes of violence and coercion.

Civil War within a Civil War

In the days when the government was putting an end to the Aragon communes, *Frente Rojo*, the Communist

MILITARIZING THE MILITIAS

In the first months after the civil war broke out, it was the political and labor union forces that organized the defense of the Republic by setting up militia columns which maintained the traits – and the insignia – of strong political cohesiveness. Among them stood out the Durruti column, led by the extremely popular anarchist commander who would be killed while defending Madrid, and the legendary Fifth Regiment, created by the Communists and headed by commanders Lister and Modesto. In a short time, however, it became apparent that the militias were not capable of resisting for long against a true army, and so the decision was made to militarize them. The army was therefore reorganized by reintegrating the most reliable professional officers, and constituting a central nucleus, the mixed brigade, composed of several infantry battalions. These were autonomous, having their own artillery, cavalry, leadership and transmission sectors. For the anarchists, who particularly hated the forms and discipline of military life, the traumatic change awakened a great deal of resistance. But the brigades essentially maintained their internal political affinities, and kept up political awareness through the institution of political commissaries, along the lines of those in the Red Army. ■

COLLECTIVIZATION IN THE COUNTRYSIDE

Collectivization was a contradictory experience, in which the enthusiastic compliance of some often coexisted with impositions suffered by others. Here, such contrasting aspects are reflected in the oral testimonies collected by the English historian, Ronald Fraser:

" – I was so enthusiastic, so fanatic that I took everything in my parents' house – all the grain stocks, the dozen head of sheep, even the silver coins – and handed them into the collective, recalled Sevilla Pastor who came from a prosperous peasant family which owned two houses and more land than they could work... So you can see I wasn't in the CNT to defend my daily wage; I was in it for idealistic reasons. My parents weren't as convinced as I, that's for sure...

" – Our next move was a mistake – the biggest of all... We obliged all right-wingers to join. Coerced them morally, not physically, but coerced them all the same...

"A band of armed men had arrived from Alcañiz, the nearest large town, 'to clean up the village in the name of the CNT.' Its first action was to arrest the local Anti-Fascist committee and take its members... to the townhall where they were locked up. The committee was accused of 'cowardice' for having refused a purge. Within a couple hours, six men had been shot...

"The incident, following on the burning of the church... posed a considerable threat. Who could tell if it might not be repeated... violence was everywhere. Within a short time, 2,000 of the village's 2,300 inhabitants had joined the collective." ■

– Fraser, R. *Blood of Spain: An Oral History of the Spanish Civil War.* New York: Pantheon, 1979. 352–353.

Party newspaper, wrote: "There is not a single Aragonese peasant who has not been forced to enter the collectives... Their lands have been taken away, and they have been made to work them from morning to night, for a salary of 95 cents. Whoever rebelled was deprived of bread, soap and everything necessary to live... Well-known, prominent fascists have taken seats on the councils."

Here, then, were the adversaries of collectivization. It may appear paradoxical that the Communists, who looked to the Soviet Union (the nation where the most thorough collectivization in the world had been achieved) as the "homeland of Socialism," were so bitterly hostile toward Spain's collectivization as to use the same tone, and the same distortion of fact, adopted by the most fervent anti-Communists. But this paradox was implicit in an even greater paradox, which embraced all the dramatic contradictions that exploded within the Republican alliance: the Spanish Communists were *against* the revolution, and they engaged all their strength in limiting it. Their slogan was "*Antes ganar la guerra*": First win the war – then we will have a revolution.

As we have seen, this position was consonant with the interests of the USSR. Things could be no different in those iron-clad times. But the position was also quite logical. Was not victory the primary aim, without which any other conquest would be lost? In order to gain victory (as the First World War had taught), was not the mobilization of the whole of society necessary, along with its total, unanimous dedication to the war effort? Didn't the revolution – especially the libertarian one, with no leader and no head – disperse energy and waste resources, creating serious contrasts among the antifascist social forces? Didn't it make the capitalist and democratic powers, whose interests were menaced, hostile to the Republic?

Such logic becomes illogical, though, if it clashes with a mass movement. In fact, the anarchist slogan – "Make a revolution to win the war" – also held some element of force and truth. How was it possible to halt the thousands of workers and peasants trained in the militias of anarchist and socialist organizations who were fighting for revolution? How could one make them accept,

The anarchist Buenaventura Durruti commanded a militia column at the Aragon front. On November 14, he led his men to Madrid to bring help from the Catalan revolution. On the 19th, while defending the city, he fell in obscure circumstances – there was some talk of a terrorist attack – and his body was returned to Barcelona accompanied by a long cortége led by President Companys and Garcia Olivier, the anarchist Minister of Justice in the Caballero government.
© Coll.Viollet/T

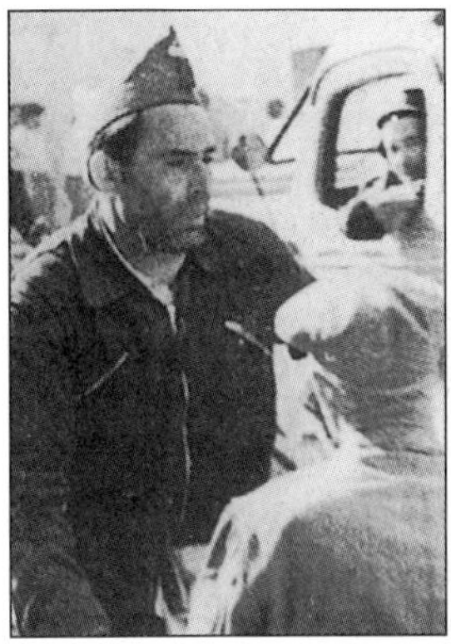

Left, armed peasants work on collectivized property.

instead, the "defense of the democratic Republic," another slogan that Communist leaders – from the party secretary, Pepe Diaz, to Dolores Ibarruri, the popular Pasionaria – were launching those days?

The democratic Republic was "of a new kind," theorized "Ercoli" (Palmiro Togliatti), who was sent to Spain by the International. And the fact that this was not an empty formula became evident when, in October 1936, Uribe, the Communist Minister of Agriculture, issued an act expropriating lands belonging to owners compromised by involvement with the military coup (virtually the majority of large and medium *terratenientes*). That act made provision for an agrarian reform of an extent never before seen in a "democratic bourgeois" system.

But in a daily life in which many peasants and day laborers, often led by their agrarian labor unions, were already exploiting the lands belonging to the collective regime, how was it possible to convince them that such a measure was not primarily meant to sabotage the revolution already in the making in the countryside?

Dolores Ibarruri, with Pepe Díaz, the secretary of the Communist Party, and Palmiro Togliatti, who, under the name of "Ercoli" was in Spain as an envoy from the Communist International. The communists countered the anarchists' slogan, "Make revolution to win the war," with their "Win the war to make revolution." They staunchly advocated "defending the democratic Republic."
© Publifoto

This conflict was made more poisonous by the fact that, by virtue of its more moderate positions, the Communist Party attracted to its ranks many members of the middle classes, whose interests, of course, began to influence the party's politics. Membership in the Communist Party (PCE) had grown considerably since prewar times, but still, its influence over the Republican government, which was due above all to the decisive amount of aid from Moscow, was disproportionate to its size. Moreover, the systematic pursuit of administrative posts and military commands, awakened hostility even among those forces which in great measure shared the PCE's orientation – including Caballero himself, as well as other parties of the Republican coalition.

As time passed, positions became more clearly defined. The Republic was incapable of organizing a military offensive, and in February 1937, Málaga fell to Franco's army. For many months, making a revolution in order to win the war had been the real strategy followed in much of Republican Spain. But the war was being lost.

The situation thus hurled toward war. And the point of collision could be none other than Barcelona, the revolutionary city, the city farthest from control by the central government. There, a small, anti-Stalinist party – the POUM (Partido Obrero de Unificacion Marxista), the object of the Communist International's greatest aversion, was attempting to orient the anarchist organizations in the direction of a political revolution along the lines of the original Russian one. This aim was sometimes foolhardy in its ambition. The English writer, George Orwell, who happened to fight in a column of the POUM, rendered the conflict almost tangible: "[U]nder the seeming gaiety of the streets, with their flower-stalls, their many-coloured flags, their propaganda-posters, and thronging crowds, there was an unmistakable and horrible feeling of political rivalry and hatred."

A single clash was therefore sufficient to spark off the decisive battle. In early May of 1937 the Catalan government police force, headed by a Communist, tried to occupy the telephone company building where the anarchists, who had been settled in there since July, con-

A *POUM (the revolutionary, anti-Stalinist, communist party aligned with the anarchists) poster and demonstration in Barcelona in February 1937. The party, which was accused of being "Trotskyist," tried, perhaps with unrealistic ambition, to model the Spanish revolution on the Soviet's, which contributed to isolating Barcelona from the central government.*
© b Publifoto

trolled all communications. A shooting match broke out and soon spread throughout the city. Barricades re-emerged, behind which on one side, the POUM militants were shooting together with the anarchists; and on the other, the Communists of the PSUC (Partit Socialita Unificat de Catalunya) together with the Catalan autonomists. The fighting caused hundreds of casualties, and was ended by appeals from the anarchist ministers who had hastened in from Madrid, followed by the intervention of central government troops sent to preside over pacification.

What followed brought total victory for the Communists. The events in Barcelona created a fine occasion for the change in government that had been gestating for several months. After the fall of Málaga, the Communists had taken up an offensive against Caballero, whom they judged to be incompetent and ever more indulgent toward the revolutionary line, just so that he could stay in power. The Communists opened the crisis after the old Socialist leader refused to agree to their request to

THE DAYS OF BARCELONA, THROUGH THE EYES OF A WRITER

Besides George Orwell, who gave ample testimony in his *Homage to Catalonia*, another English writer, John Langdon-Davies, has left us a live report of the Barcelona battles of May 1937. Although the political bent of his writings was, as Orwell accused, too uncritically Communist, his description of the strange coexistence between war and peace during those days is extraordinarily vivid.

"The burst of shots coming from the area of the Carlo Marx Casal could mean either an attack from the street side, or an attack of nerves on the part of those who were in there. Since silence then followed, it had probably been an attack of nerves.

"We raise the blinds and go out into the street. The woman selling newspapers continued to stand motionlessly beneath the street lamp; not a soul passed, except for some factory workers hastening toward their workplaces or to their union headquarters, to receive orders. We stop and talk. A car goes by and disappears at full speed in the direction of the Diagonal. It seemed as if the wheels were crumbling invisible biscuits, and if its passage were greeted by rifle shots from buildings immersed in darkness. A burst of shots rings out from very nearby. We keep up the appearance of indifference, but retreat toward the entrance to the restaurant. The newspaper woman does the same. It is a curious thing – I've thought about it all week long – how people take cover after a burst of gunfire, when the danger has passed, and take up doing what they were doing, after a moment of silence, when a new burst of shots may come…

"After a moment, the lady comes out of invisibility and sits down at her place, folds some newspapers and goes back to her immobility, for lack of customers." ■

– Langdon-Davies, J. *La setmana tragica de 1937*. Barcelona: Edicions 62, 1987. 152–153.

dissolve the POUM; they succeeded in imposing a new government which excluded the anarchists. That government was supported by the Republican parties and by Prieto's moderate Socialists, and headed by one of the latter, Juan Negrín. In the face of this brusque change in direction, the Socialist Left and the anarchists protested. But they could do nothing more than make noise, for the military incapacity of Caballero's government was all too evident, as was the revolutionaries' inability to make war and revolution simultaneously.

The POUM was outlawed; its leaders were imprisoned; its secretary, Andrés Nin, was kidnapped and assassinated. In August the Aragon Council was dissolved, and the Fifth Regiment of the army, commanded by the Communist, Enrique Lister, occupied the region and began to break up the collectives. At the end of October, the Negrín government, with the chief aim of directly promoting an efficient war industry, moved to Barcelona; the move strongly limited Catalan autonomy.

Finance Minister in the Caballero government, the Socialist physioloist Juan Negrín (left), one of the most well-known professors at the university of Madrid, became head of the government in the spring of 1937, after the Barcelona conflict between anarchists, communists and Catalan separatists brought about the demise of Caballero.
© Publifoto

Militiamen leaving for the Aragon front march down the streets of Barcelona.
© Sergi i Octavi Centelles

Chapter 4

THE RISE OF FRANCO AND THE BIRTH OF HIS REGIME

MILITARY CONTROL BEHIND NATIONALIST LINES IS TOTAL. BUT WHO ARE THESE DEFENDERS OF THE "OTHER" SPAIN, AND WHAT ARE THEY FIGHTING FOR? AND HOW CAN FRANCO UNITE THE DIFFERENT TENDENCIES OF THE NEW *RECONQUISTA*?

Behind the lines of the Nationalist front was a very different scene from the one in the Republican zone. Takeover by the military had been total. All the different right-wing political forces were subordinate to the army. The elimination of all opponents was complete. From the very beginning, however, a leadership problem had existed, since General Sanjurjo, who had been chosen by the conspirators as head of the insurrection, died in the crash of the airplane that had been carrying him home from Portugal. Moreover, since the coup was growing into a long civil war, there was the problem of forming a government capable of facing such a war. And in the background there also emerged an institutional question, because the political forces, and to some degree the military as well, who were united in their intent to dissolve the Popular Front, were divided between support for a republic or a monarchy. To further complicate matters, the monarchists were divided into two groups: the *alfonsinas*, who advocated the restoration to power of King Alfonso XIII, and the *carlistas*, who supported another dynastic branch.

At any rate, everything was decided within army circles, and the criterion for making a choice was fundamentally military: Which had the most chance of leading them to victory? The designation of Franco was almost taken for granted, and not surprisingly, it was made rapidly, and with little opposition. Of the four generals who, according to a very popular Republican song, were destined to hang on Christmas Eve – Cabanellas, Mola,

***A** poster with the portrait of Franco, pasted up in the Nationalist zone after his appointment as Head of State. At first, Franco did not belong to the National Defense Junta, a sort of generic directing body instituted by the coup forces and headed (after Sanjurjo's death) by the general of highest rank, Miguel Cabanellas. When the coup forces were faced with the problem of a long war, in order to consolidate power in a single voice, they appointed Franco "Head of Government of the Spanish State" on September 29, 1936.*

Franco and General Emilio Mola enter Burgos in October 1936. Mola, who was one of the main perpetrators of the conspiracy, died in a plane accident on June 3, 1937, while engaged with his northern army in putting down Basque resistance. As had happened with Sanjurjo, a banal accident eliminated one of Franco's potential rivals for power.
© Publifoto

Queipo de Llano and Franco – the latter was the one who could offer a combination of military prowess, command of the African army, and the trust of Germany and Italy. And he was also a clever politician, unlike his companions. Immersed in military logic, they turned absolute political power over to him, as if it were a necessary appendage to his title of Generalísimo, the supreme commander of operations. At the end of September 1936, they designated him as "Head of Chiefs of Staff" and attributed all powers to him. Few realized that Franco would be reluctant to give up those powers – not even Cabanellas, who abstained from voting, nor Mola, who expressed his own reservations.

From Generalísimo to Caudillo

It is difficult to establish whether or not Franco, as some have suggested, subordinated the course of the war to the consolidation of his own power. It is certainly true that he delayed the advance on Madrid, perhaps in such a way as to jeopardize its victorious outcome, in order to stop and liberate the Alcázar of Toledo, where cadets faithful to him had long been under siege. This episode, celebrated by right-wing elements all over the world, gained him such prestige and popularity as to garner support for his consolidation of power. It is also true that the long war – too long, even in the opinion of his protectors, Hitler and Mussolini – was destined to magnify his savior's halo in the eyes of those who had suffered or feared captivity and persecution in the "red zone." Such prestige would serve him as protection at the most difficult moments of his long regime.

Striving toward power with all his strength, and convinced of his mission, Franco, however, was not devoid of values: they were and remained those common to traditionalists all over the world, summarized in the triad "God, country and family," and accompanied by a social conservatism that was not as rigid as some. These values certainly did not delineate any precise political ideology. Like many military politicians in Europe between the two world wars, Franco, too – in a definition coined by the historian, Arno Mayer – was "a bayonet in search of an ideology." Admiration, opportunism and imitation

After the insurrection failed, about 1,000 men, including civil police, assault soldiers, Falangists and cadets entrenched themselves behind the walls of the Alcazár, the fort in Toledo that dominates the Tagus River. They were liberated on September 26, after ten weeks of siege, by the African army. The following day, Colonel Moscardo (fourth from left), commander of the resistance, reported "Sin novedad" *(nothing new).*
© Publifoto

THE ALCÁZAR EPIC

One war episode in Spain that Franco's propaganda managed to magnify in world opinion was the long resistance of the Alcazár, the military academy of Toledo, where cadets had taken refuge along with their military instructors and families. The epic, legendary version of the facts did not mention the detail that the victims of the siege had forced many hostages to follow them, and held them prisoner within the walls. Instead, the account insisted on the commander's sacrifice; Colonel Muscardó is said to have allowed the shooting of his son, who was captured by the "reds," rather than surrender the fort in exchange for the son's life. In reality, as the American historian, Herbert R. Southworth, has shown, that episode was an invention inspired by other legendary stories. What really happened was considerably less heroic. Moscardó deliberately exploited the presence of women and children in order to create problems for the aggressors, and the shooting of his son occurred later, during reprisals for an air raid. The episode became widely known in literary chronicles, including the famous "instant book" by the French writers, Henri Massis and Robert Brassilach (*Les cadets de l'Alcazár*, 1936). The 1940 film, *L'assedio dell'Alcazar,* directed by the Italian, Augusto Genina, distorted the famous Republican slogan "*¡No pasaran!* " in favor of the siege victims. ■

Below, two Nationalist propaganda posters. Included among the fundamental laws of the regime, the Fuero del Trabajo contained certain elements that would remain constant during Franco's rule: unions are "instruments in the service of the State," labor is an "obligatory tribute to national wealth," strikes, considered to be "antipatriotic crimes," are prohibited.

thus drove him in the direction of the fascist model inspired and recommended by the powers protecting him.

His personal mark, his militarist background, would become evident from the very beginning, and would always characterize his regime (it would, after all, be called Francoist). The only party, founded at Franco's command in April 1937, was a hybrid mix of the Falange and the Carlists' Comunión Tradicionalista. These two movements were absolutely extraneous to each other and would always remain hostile to one another. They were held together by the person of the Caudillo, who, according to statute, impersonated "all the values and all the honors (of the party) as the author of the historical era in which Spain acquired the possibility of achieving its destiny."

The Carlists and the Falange were chosen to create the new party instead of other, larger right-wing parties, such as the CEDA or the Alfonsine monarchists, because they had armed militias. The Carlist Requeté was made up mainly of Navarrese volunteers. Preventively subordinated to the military hierarchy, like that of the Falange, this militia was thus removed from the sphere of influence of Franco's potential rival, General Mola. The Requeté – about 30,000 men – had until then constituted the strong nucleus of Mola's army, which was based in Navarra.

Complaints and resistance within the original move-

THE FUERO DEL TRABAJO

Above and beyond its title, the Fuero del Trabajo or "work forum," which later would become a basic law of the State, intended to expound the fundamental doctrinal principles of the regime.
But the desire to unite inspiring principles of various origins produced a strange juxtaposition of grandiloquent terms, a junk bag of confused, inconsistent concepts, and bits and pieces of different ideologies and traditions, as can be seen in the preamble itself: "Renewing the Catholic Tradition of social justice with the profound humanitarian sense that inspired our Imperial legislation, the national State, as a totalitarian instrument at the service of the Fatherland's integrity, and as an instrument of unionism, in that it represents a reaction against liberal capitalism and Marxist materialism, undertakes the mission of achieving – according to a custom which is military, constructive and highly religious – the revolution that Spain began, and which must restore to Spaniards, once and for all, the Fatherland, Bread and Justice." ■

Instituto de Estudios políticos, *Leyes políticas de España*. Madrid, 1956. 40.

ments were suffocated. Fal Conde, the leader of the Carlists, who jealously hoped to maintain the autonomy of his movement, was exiled as a precautionary measure. The discontented members of the Falange were led briefly by Manuel Hedilla – the proto-Nazi who had succeeded José Antonio as party head after he had been executed in the Republican zone; they made several protest demonstrations in Salamanca, the Caudillo's headquarters. They were soon arrested and tried before the war counsel. Hedilla, who was initially sentenced to death, had his sentence commuted to house arrest in the Canary Islands, only because of intervention on his behalf by Faupel, the German ambassador.

Ramon Serrano Suñer (seventh from the left), state lawyer, parliamentary representative of the CEDA, and Franco's brother-in-law, arrived in Salamanca in February 1937, after escaping the zone controlled by the Republican government. From then on he was dedicated to giving governmental form to the Generalísimo's ideas, by creating the institutions necessary to channel and widen Franco's authority.
© Publifoto

Fascistization was no doubt a necessary instrument for Franco. In this effort he was directly inspired by his brother-in-law, Ramon Serrano (whom popular irony would place at the Generalísimo's side with the title of "Cuñadísimo"). Indeed, his burgeoning regime did not want to be defined by the opposition only in negative terms: anti-Marxist, anti-liberal, and so forth. But above and beyond the Unification Act and exterior changes – Falange uniforms and symbols were widespread throughout the national zone – the new party's role remained marginal. During the course of the war, the Falange's totalitarian attempt to infiltrate society did not go beyond an active presence in the Female Sector, which was directed by Pilar Primo de Rivera, the founder's sister. The Sector created a network of canteens, food distribution centers, and infirmary services at the front and behind front lines.

Not much was done even in terms of the regime's ide-

For God, for Country
and for King
they fought against
our fathers.
For God, for Country
and for King
we, too, shall fight.
We shall all fight
together,
in unity, together
to defend the flag
of holy tradition.
– Song of the Requetés

ological and institutional formation. Franco was particularly insensitive to this element. He limited himself to pronouncing a few principles contained in the March 1938 *Fuero del Trabajo*, whose very title betrays its direct affiliation with Mussolini's *Carta del Lavoro*. The Spanish text, unlike the Italian one, reflected a need to satisfy the different components of the *Movimiento* (this term came to be preferred over "party," which smacked of liberal roots). To this end it presented a particularly vague mixture of productivism, unionism and evocations of traditional values.

At any rate, the *Fuero del Trabajo* and the *Carta del Lavoro* were essentially similar. They both subordinated producers of goods to the aims of the State, and thus – in practice – to the dictator who was its interpreter. No sympathy for the plight of the working masses had contributed to the formation of Franco's character. He was strictly a military man who preferred military values, such as hierarchy and obedience. So much so, that several theoreticians of the new regime, in adapting it to the Generalísimo's character traits, spoke of a new category: *caudillaje*, a sort of Spanish Caesarian militarism.

The Cruzada

The imitative, contingent nature of Spanish fascism must not lead one to believe that the Nationalist zone was pervaded only by feelings of indifference and terror. On the contrary: it was also pervaded by authentic fervor, by a strong sense of sacrifice and dedication to the cause. But at the root of such emotional involvement was not the fascist ideology, but faith – the crusader spirit. *Cruzada* soon came to indicate, in summarized form, the culmination of the *alzamiento*: safeguarding the faith (in its highly Spanish version) and the Church. One cannot really understand the reasons for Franco's victory without considering the fact that his cause was identified with the Church. Not only did the Church give Franco's struggle deep religious and spiritual motivations, not only did it win over strong international support, which was sustained by Papal authority and the Vatican, but most importantly, it drew many Spanish Catholics into the fray. They became the base upon which the regime stood.

None of this was at all implicit in the military insurrection itself. In the proclamations that accompanied the coup, no emphasis was given to any dangers menacing the Church. At first, Franco did not mention any such dangers at all. But the spontaneous, fierce popular anticlericalism that immediately exploded in the Republican zone complicated the conflict. It mixed the politico-social motivations of both fronts with religious motivations, ennobling the military's civil war by presenting it as a war in defense of religion. "If today's conflict," wrote Cardinal Goma, primate of Spain, "may appear as a purely civil war, since it is fought by Spaniards themselves on Spanish soil, when all is said and done we must recognize in it a true crusader spirit, in support of the Catholic religion."

Blessing of a Francoist cavalry division in Valladolid (© Publifoto) and a church transformed into headquarters for militia in the Republican zone.

In the beginning the war was not at all what Cardinal Goma described, but events in the Republican zone soon gave legitimacy to his words. A destructive flood, a demolishing fever, spread everywhere – in cities, in towns, in the remotest corners – against churches, chapels, convents and any other ecclesiastical building. Nor was damage limited to the burning and tearing down of buildings; nearly everywhere, iconoclastic fervor destroyed images, church furnishings, books, relics. Many local committees confiscated images and objects of worship in the possession of private individuals, and burned those symbols of "friar domination" in public bonfires.

The anticlerical furor, which turned into a wholesale persecution against all Catholics, struck indiscriminately. Nearly 7,000 were victims, according to reliable estimates. This count is much less than figures presented in written and spoken propaganda during wartime (in his *Aux martyrs espagnols*, Paul Claudel spoke of 16,000 victims). But it does give an idea of a human sacrifice of enormous proportion. In the Barbastro diocese, for example, a shocking 88 percent of clergymen were eliminated, along with 66 percent in the Lérida diocese and 62 percent in Tolosa. The large urban dioceses were also struck cruelly: in Madrid, 334 priests were killed (30 percent); in Barcelona, 279 (22 percent); in Valencia, 327 (27 percent).

Below, Franco's triumph depicted in a portrait by Ignacio Zuloaga. Standard bearer of the new Reconquista *against atheist Spain, Franco combined the different symbols of nationalism: he is wearing the red cap of the Requeté, the Carlist armed militia, and the uniform of the Falange; on his chest we see the yoke and arrows of the Catholic kings who achieved the first* Reconquista.

To present these facts as the result of a deliberate policy carried out by the Republican authorities amounted to a rallying cry for Franco's forces. As hostile to the Church as the Republican authorities were, they were perfectly aware of how much this violence harmed the Republic. But in the first months, a period in which much anti-Catholic hatred flamed up and burned, the authorities – as we have seen – were absolutely incapable of exercising any control over the popular movement. Nor were they later able to do much more than halt persecution: too deep was the split that divided Spanish society over the theme of religion, too poisoned the atmosphere by all the blood that had been shed, to allow a return to normal practices of worship (though some government leaders would have wished it so). With the exception of the Basque region, where the local Republican authorities were mostly Catholic, and the Church's support for Basque nationalism brought it closer to the people and protected it from any persecution, the civil war left democratic Catholics no choice. One of these, the Catalan priest, Carles Cardo wrote: "One of the warring parties kills us, and the other defends us... Who can be surprised that those who were persecuted, and who barely managed to escape death, chose the other side?"

Right, a Nationalist poster publicizes the idea of the war as a crusade.

The "inevitable error" thus produced its most poisonous fruit. An old-style *pronunciamiento*, with its blind aversion to democracy and its stubborn hostility toward the emancipation of the peasant masses, thus succeeded in hiding under the mantle of a religious war, calling even generous souls to arms; it succeeded in awakening a state of religious-patriotic exaltation that created a heroic will to combat. It would therefore be a mistake to limit oneself to the image focused on by Republican propaganda: fat prelates making the Roman salute or blessing the weapons of Franco's coup forces. In the Nationalist zone, it was more frequent to see armies of young people reciting fervent rosaries together, or singing religious hymns in a chorus before going off to the battlefield for the "holy war"; they marched on, their shirts adorned with sacred images, animated to the point of fanaticism by the spirit of sacrifice.

THE CHURCH IN THE REPUBLICAN ZONE

In a memorandum presented to the Council of Ministers in January 1937, the Catholic, Manuel Irujo, then minister without portfolio representing the Basque Nationalist Party in the Caballero government, denounced the gravity and extent of religious persecution in the Republican zone. We present here his most significant passage.

"The real situation of the Church throughout the territory under Republican control, except for the Basque territory, has been the following since last July:

1) All altars, images and objects of worship, with very few exceptions, have been destroyed, usually with vilification.

2) All churches have been closed to worship. Public worship is therefore entirely suspended.

3) A great number of churches – the norm in Catalunya – have been set on fire.

4) Deposits and warehouses belonging to official organizations contained collections of bells, chalices, reliquaries, candelabra and other sacred objects, which were then melted down and utilized in the war or for industrial ends.

5) Deposits of all kinds, as well as markets, garages, stables, refuges and rooms for various uses... have been set up in churches.

6) All convents have been evacuated, and religious community life suspended. Their buildings, sacred objects and all types of possessions have been set afire, sacked, occupied or destroyed.

7) Thousands of priests and other Catholics have been arrested, imprisoned and shot without trial...

8) They have gone so far as to prohibit the private possession of sacred objects and images. The police carry out searches in homes, violating the intimate personal or family life within; with scorn they violently destroy images, prints, religious books and everything having to do with worship." ■

– Manent, A. & Raventos, J. *L'esglesia clandestina a Catalunya durante la guerra civil (1936–1939)*. Montserrat, 1984. 22–23.

The *Cruzada* was not only instrumental in reviving glories long past, but it provided a patina that covered up the history of the church's treatment of the masses.

The price, gladly paid by the Caudillo to the Church in exchange for its essential support, was his renunciation of any personal pretext at totalitarianism (a totalitarianism that, at any rate, he would have been incapable of expressing or exercising). The Church was thus fully entrusted with the education, formation and morals of the populace. The ecclesiastical environment would long be dominated by the most traditionalist, backward elements. Confessionalism and clericalism were the strongest mediating forces in civil society, while schoolrooms, public spectacles, courtrooms, and means of communication, were clearly under constant tutelage by the Church. The precepts of the faithful were confused with civil duty. But in time, when the memory of war was remote and the Church had changed direction in many ways, the role it had assumed during the regime would become one of its weakest points.

In the Nationalist zone, armed peasants escort a religious procession.

FRANCO'S SCHOOLS

An example of the Church's domination of the Nationalist zone can be seen in the directives given by the Commission for Culture and Instruction appointed by Franco to "regenerate" public schooling. Among the new norms established, one especially notes those intending to introduce the exercise of Catholic devotional practices among the scholastic obligations of teachers and students alike.

Here is an example, in a norm issued in the Official State Bulletin of April 10, 1937:

1) In all schools there must be an image of the Holy Virgin, preferably with the very Spanish title of Immaculate Conception. It will be the task of teachers to arrange for this according to the measure of their zeal, by placing the image in a special place.

2) During the month of May, according to age-old Spanish custom, teachers will do the exercises of the Marian month, together with their students, before said image.

3) Every day of the year, upon entering and leaving school, students will give the greeting as our fathers did, saying "Hail Purest Mary," and the teacher will respond, "Conceived without sin." ■

– Díaz-Plaja, F. *La guerra de España en sus documentos*. Barcelona: Plaza & Janés, 1973. 283.

The New *Reconquista*

In this crusader spirit, Franco tried to depict his war as a renewal of the ancient *Reconquista*, the centuries-long process by which Spanish Christians had progressively taken territory from the Moors, and thus from Islam. This time, Moorish assault troops were on the side of the "new crusaders," but except for this obvious contradiction, the real development of the war justified the comparison.

The Nationalists did not succeed in reaching Madrid. And all successive attempts at surrounding the city and interrupting its roads were defeated. So they went on the road to La Coruña, where the offensive conducted by General Orgaz between December 1936 and January 1937 was halted before the Nationalist army was able to reach its tactical goals. So it went in the battle of the Jarama river, which Orgaz led a few months later, hoping to interrupt communications between Madrid and Valencia. So it went in the battle of Guadalajara, in whose zone Franco opened a great offensive in March 1937, aimed at encircling the capital, a bold maneuver that relied basically on the speed of the 40,000 strong motorized Italian troops commanded by General Roatta. When these troops were stuck in the mud and hit by rain, yet another operation ended in resounding defeat. In its psychological effects and the echo it sent out internationally, it was transformed into the Republic's most important victory.

Italian tanks advance toward the Guadalajara front. Italian involvement in Spain was even greater than German involvement. During the course of the war, about 73,000 Italians fought beside the Francoists, as well as another 4,000 in aviation. The navy blockaded Republican ports with 149 units, which included the submarines necessary to intercept naval supplies headed for the Republic.

The defeat at Guadalajara finally forced Franco to abandon his attempts to attack the capital, thus diverting operations over the rest of the country. But as early as February 1937, before Guadalajara, the Nationalists had retaken Málaga, and the Republican army seemed incapable of launching any important attacks. This failure was a result of the greatly reduced Republican force,

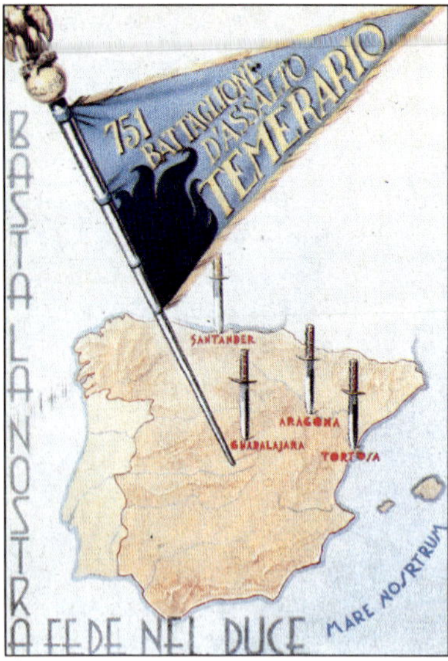

but it was also surely influenced by a new phenomenon: the direct intervention by those Italian troops, (even if they did end up performing so poorly in Guadalajara).

Having lost the battle of Madrid, the Fascist powers had, in fact, decided to expand their involvement, ignoring the pledge of "non-intervention." But while Germany, intent on not becoming involved in war before completing its own armament program, was limited to increasing weapon supplies, Italy proceeded to take up a direct form of intervention from which it hoped to gain great advantages for its position in the Mediterranean. After January 1937, about 70,000 men enrolled in the CTV, or "volunteer corps troops" (though most were not volunteers at all), were sent to Spain. And Mussolini did not limit himself to sending men, but also airplanes, complete with pilots, cannons, mortars and other war supplies, all of which were dispensed without much concern for any financial compensation.

THE BATTLE OF GUADALAJARA:

The battle of Guadalajara, one of the first experiments in modern mobility warfare, ended in disastrous failure. The essential phases are presented here by the Spanish historian Cardon:

"The operation, planned for the last days of winter, had been calculated in its finest details. It was based on the boldness and velocity of motorized columns, supported by artillery and the air force, like the war operations that a few years later would be carried out by the German army in the Blitzkrieg. On the whole, this was a modern, ambitious offensive within the context of the slow, primitive Spanish war. Its first attack it would be carried out in a parallel manner by two Italian divisions: one along the main road, and the other in the direction of secondary roads... When the Italians arrived at Alcalá they would place themselves behind the Republicans, who were just back from the Jarama battle. At that point the Nationalists would attack... squeezing the Republicans between two lines of fire.

"At 7 o'clock on the morning of March 8, the first shots resounded from the Italian cannons. But the attacking forces found themselves facing an unexpected problem. Unusually for the climate during that time of year, it was raining. With the rain, the clay-laden soil of Alcarria had become a muddy marsh; the airports, their runways heavily damaged by mud puddles, were closed; the artillery, whose observatories were blinded, lost sight of their objectives. The Italian vanguard attacked the front-line Republicans. Surprise was total; positions had to be abandoned. It took the Republican command several hours to understand where its forces had ended up. Then it took up the resources left to it. Tiredly, the worn-out Jarama units marched along to Guadalajara...

"On the next day, while the Republicans were in confusion, trying to find points from which to set up their resistance efforts, the Italians kept on advancing. Their speed was less than had been foreseen, as the weather had gotten worse, but everything was proceeding well enough... From that moment

Yet the contribution of the Italian troops to Franco's victory was often underestimated – perhaps because of their initial ineffectiveness in the battle of Guadalajara, perhaps because the Franco regime downplayed the importance of foreign assistance, or maybe even because the guilty consciences of those who advocated "non-intervention" required that denial. In the context of this war, however, in which neither of the sides shone with any particular military strength, a large, relatively well-equipped expedition corps like the Italian one could not help but be influential. Indeed, it would be a protagonist – sometimes a decisive one – in all the most important war actions, beginning with the campaign in the north, which was soon to follow.

Two postcards commemorating Italian intervention in Spain.

After Guadalajara, during the spring of 1937, the Nationalists carried out a lengthy offensive throughout the Basque country. From the east, Mola's Navarrese troops, supported by the Italian "Frecce Nere," slowly but progressively invaded the territory. The dif-

THE DEFEAT OF FASCISM

on, the motorized operation was to begin... On the following day the Italian maneuvers continued, but they were thrown into a state of disorganization by the bad weather. In the sea of mud, whoever went off the road was trapped; the artillery and air forces could not bring support, because of the lack of visibility; the men were soaking wet and freezing. The road was transformed into a great knot of units and vehicles getting in each other's way. The men of the Third Italian Division were demoralized by the cold, the continuous rain and a march which became slower and slower, with no support nor reinforcements... Amid growing disquietude, the Garibaldi battalion of the Twelfth International Brigade threw wood on the fire of discontent. These were Italians – exiled antifascists who had hastened into Spain to fight the man whom they considered Mussolini's political cousin. They turned to their compatriots with all the propaganda means at their disposal. An offensive made by proclamations and loudspeakers targeted the CTV units. Amid the cold and the discouragement, many volunteers heard the warm invitation in their own language, coming from the opposing trenches. In the Italian corps, men began to desert... the Italian command decided that that night, the divisions of the second grouping would replace those of the first, who were tired and longing for rest. After sunset, this substitution was ordered. It was a touchy operation. The first-line units were supposed to wait for those behind the lines to arrive... and retreat without the enemy noticing. That is not how it went. Pressed by the Republicans, the front-line troops were unable to wait. Before the replacements arrived, the soldiers began to retreat. They abandoned their weapons in the muddy soil and started assaulting trucks going away from the front. The following morning, the Republicans took advantage of the occasion. They attacked, and the Italian defeat became total." ■

– Cardon, G. "Las operaciones militares," in Vari, *La guerra civil espanola: 50 años después.* Barcelona: Labor, 1986. 226–229.

ference in strength between the conflicting sides lay in aviation.

Mola's army could count on continuous support from German and Italian aviation forces, which successfully tried out new tactics of collaboration between air and land divisions, as well as proving the efficacy of terrorist bombings in the cities (Durango and Guérnica were entirely destroyed). At the same time, Basques under the direct command of the autonomous army gained late, partial and sporadic aid from the Republican air force. But the attempts made by the latter to stop the Nationalists by attacking on the Madrid Sierra and on the Aragonese front, were weak and of short duration, while dissension between politicians and the military impaired the launching of the planned massive Estremadura offensive.

Departure of a convoy of Francoist soldiers for the front, just before the spring of 1937 offensive that, after the Guadalajara defeat, led to the conquest of northern Spain. © Publifoto

Basque resistance became desperate. On June 3, 1937 General Mola died in a plane crash. But this did not stop the offensive. In fact, as the German ambassador, Faupel, wrote to Berlin: "After the death of General Mola, the Generalísimo seems visibly more at ease in directing

THE ITALIAN CONTRIBUTION, ACCORDING TO QUEIPO DE LLANO

In October 1938 General Queipo de Llano made a farewell speech addressed to a contingent of Italian soldiers about to return to their homeland. In his words one can note both the pompous minimization of the Italian effort, and the vulgarity of accusations made toward the adversary. "You did not come to Spain because your presence was indispensable in order to fight and conquer the miserable individuals paid by Moscow, who wanted to ruin their country itself and turn it over to the Jews, because we had more than enough strength to win. You came to fight for an ideal, and the reason why you came is the solidarity among men who are repelled and horrified by the ideas of Stalin. Your arrival was the logical answer to the Reds standing outside the walls of Madrid, where the International Brigades gathered, composed of the dregs of the European peoples, who did not come to fight as you did – for an ideal – but to satisfy their plundering instincts, proper to those who dreamed up the Popular Front." ■

– Díaz-Plaja, *La guerra de España en sus documentos.* Barcelona: Plaza & Janés, 1973. 556.

operations." On June 12, the Navarrese brigades, supported by 70 bombers and 50 fighter planes, broke through the so-called "iron belt," the defensive strip protecting Bilbao. Help arrived late from the west – from Asturias and Santander, also blocked by the attackers, and by the sea. A week later, Navarrese and Italian troops entered the capital of Biscay, and on June 23, Franco punished the "Basque rebels" with a decree abrogating the autonomy statute, as well as the fiscal privileges that the Basque country had enjoyed for centuries.

What remained of the Republican North now had no escape. In July, the Negrín government, with its new head of state, General Vicente Rojo, launched an offensive against Brunete, in the area near Madrid. It was an important undertaking, in which 50,000 men and 150 tanks were involved. But the strategic goal of occupying positions meant to halt the Nationalist forces in the north for a lengthy period of time, failed. The battle gained nothing more than a delay in the final conquest of the north. In mid-August, six Navarrese brigades and three Italian divisions, supported from the air by the infamous Condor Legion, attacked Santander. They entered the city on the July 26.

Then it was Asturias' turn. This operation, too, was delayed by a Republican offensive that was launched on the Aragon front, where 80,000 men, commanded by General Pozas, attacked in the Belchite district, aiming to threaten Saragossa, and, again, disperse the forces of Franco's army in the north. The bloody battle, fought largely house-to-house in the little Aragonese town, ended in a few measly territorial gains for the Republican army, and failed to accomplish the strategic goals it had set.

In fact, the operation did not block Franco's south-to-west advance against the Asturian hills.

Here, the Republican forces were considerably inferior in men and means to those of the aggressor. They had severe weapons shortages and serious problems getting

Navarrese volunteers of the Requeté made up the strong nucleus of the army that broke the resistance in the Republican north. The Requeté corps, with its characteristic red beret (though during the war its men often wore the army's khaki-colored berets), had been formed during the Carlist War, 1872–1876.
© Publifoto

supplies. But they held out for a long time until, in early October, the Navarrese and Italian forces, pushing through the opening provided by the German aviators, broke through the lines and progressively occupied the region until Gijón fell. From north to south, Franco now held an uninterrupted band of territory. He had conquered ports, industries, and mineral resources. The Republic had lost them.

In August 1937 men fight house-to-house in Belchite, on the Aragon front. The district was still governed by the Aragon Council, which was controlled by the anarchists. Partly in view of the offensive against Quinto-Belchite, the Negrín government dissolved the Council in order to assure stricter governmental control over war operations. The bloody offensive led only to modest results.
© Sergi i Octavi Centelles

The *Reconquista* paused for a moment. While Franco prepared a new offensive, concentrating efforts around Guadalajara in order to re-attempt a takeover of Madrid, at the end of the year Rojo again took the initiative for the Republicans by launching an attack on Teruel. This Aragonese city constituted one of the major points of penetration by the Nationalists. Attacking Teruel seemed a limited goal, little more than a distraction, but it succeeded in derailing Franco's plans. After hard combat in the heart of the city, carried out in punishing cold and snow, on January 8, 1938 the Republicans won the city. But Franco's counter-offensive was not long in coming. From early February on, he sent out fifteen divisions to the attack – 125,000 men and 400 cannons. At the end of the month, after tough battles, the city was nearly surrounded, and the occupying forces were forced to abandon it. The Republican army, sorely tried and run down in its morale, thus took up its former positions.

Franco did not stop there. In early March he began preparing a new attack of huge proportions. Rojo, who had presented his resignation to no avail, was informed of this ahead of time; but in the face of such a vast front, he had no way of knowing where to plan for the attack. In the end, it was once more on the Aragon front, in the Belchite area, that the great Nationalist offensive was concentrated; it broke through the Republican lines on several points. Half the entire army was involved, along with the Italian expedition corps and 400 airplanes. The Republican army succeeded in reorganizing along a new line of defense, but the spirit of resistance had been weakened. People in cities far from the front were afraid, too. On March 16 and 17 Barcelona, which until then had been spared by the war, was bombed by Italian aircraft; such heavy bombing of a civilian population had never been heard of before. The massacre horrified the world; but Mussolini, as Ciano, his Foreign Minister, noted, declared that he was "happy for the fact that Italians are able to awaken horror for their aggressiveness rather than pleasure for their skill as mandolin players."

Rations are distributed behind Nationalist lines. It is women's participation on the Republican side of the civil war that is especially memorable: the figure of the female militia fighter became one of the symbols of the Spanish war. In the crusade-like atmosphere of the Nationalist side, women had a different place: they were valued for the family values they were thought to embody.
© Publifoto

The Defense Minister, Prieto, was unable to hide his despair, and foresaw a rapid defeat. He expressed his pessimism to other ministers and to the diplomats of other countries. Dissension within the Negrín government became acute. Together with union leadership, the Communists in Barcelona promoted a vast demonstration of popular resistance and demanded the removal of Prieto. In early April, after the formation of a new government, Prieto was replaced as head of the ministry by Negrín himself.

But this was certainly not enough. At the end of March 1938, Franco's army again took up the offensive. And this time it struck Catalunya as well. In early April, Lérida and Balaguer fell. A resistance front was formed once more. But in the south – in Aragon, as before – a new breakthrough was made in Republican defense lines, so that on April 15, the troops of Colonel Alonso Vega's Fourth Navarrese division reached the Mediterranean. A wedge formed, which would soon grow, tearing the Republican territory in two.

Chapter 5

THE HORRORS OF CIVIL WAR

EVERY CIVIL WAR LOWERS THE COMBATANTS' LEVEL OF CIVILIZED BEHAVIOR. THE SPANISH WAR WAS NO EXCEPTION. THE VIOLENCE AND HORROR THAT NEITHER SIDE SEEMED CAPABLE OF ESCAPING PREFIGURED THE TOTAL WAR THAT WAS ABOUT TO SWALLOW ALL OF EUROPE.

The various epics of heroic deeds and the starkness of the conflict in values – a Crusade (from one side's point of view) and the defense of democracy against the attack of international fascism (from the other side's perspective) – often distract one from the fact that the Spanish war was also a horrible civil war. In modern times, no country of western Europe had seen such destruction: The violence went beyond the bounds of the State's law and enforcement function and even beyond the norms regulating war between countries. Not only politics and ideologies clashed on Spanish soil, but also traditions and innovations concerning violence itself. In this respect, too, the Spanish war was a precursor: before the eyes of the world, mixing civil war and war between foreign armies, it was an early sample of the total war that was soon to come.

The exhumed mummies of Carmelite nuns are exposed to the curiosity and scorn of the inhabitants of Barcelona, at the portal of the convent church. The civil war brought forth popular anticlericalism (which had already found expression in Spain in bloody episodes during the Tragic Week of 1909): at the moment when the Republic was proclaimed (two Madrid churches were burned), and during the Asturias revolt of 1934.

"Dirty Work" and "Cleansing"

Many tales of atrocities accompanied the events of the war. Mutilation, torture, macabre jeering before executions. Men crucified, castrated, dismembered, and gored like bulls in the ring before being shot; women raped and decapitated, blown up like tires until their intestines exploded. History wavers in the face of such episodes. In part it records them, in part it drives them back into the realm of hearsay, or attributes them to propaganda meant to denigrate the enemy.

It is often impossible to disentangle facts from

hearsay and defamatory propaganda, or real violence from imagined violence. Indeed, false atrocities are a weapon of war. They awaken implacable hate and thirst for violence; they win over international public opinion to the cause of the victims. Arthur Koestler, in his *Invisible Writing*, left an enlightening testimony of how propaganda in favor of the Republic built up horrendous crimes to attribute to the enemy (and, we might add, the other side was equally good at fabricating tales). But it is also true that every civil war lowers the level of civilization, unleashing passions of death disguised as political passions, so that as far as horrors are concerned, the separating wall between what is true and what is credible becomes thin, almost imperceptible.

Federico García Lorca wearing the badge of the Barraca, the university theater group organized by the writer in 1932 on behalf of the Ministry of Public Instruction. If the participation of intellectuals in the civil war was symbolically opened by Lorca's murder in July 1936, then it closed with the death of the poet, Antonio Machado, in February 1939, a few days after he had crossed the French border.
© Publifoto

During the Spanish Civil War, people killed off the battlefield were usually summarily executed, mostly by being shot. On the front, too – after the battle had ended – very often, no prisoners were taken; instead, the captured soldiers were immediately shot. There was no respect even for the wounded. In the Nationalist camp, the Moors of the *Tercio* were often assigned the "dirty work" of "cleaning up" the camp infirmaries – generally by using knives or, as in Toledo, hand grenades. But it was usually behind the lines that true mass executions took place.

The aims declared by the coup forces and the Republican authorities regarding their adversaries' lives were very different. The Nationalists repeatedly proclaimed the will to annihilate the enemy; while the Republicans showed conciliatory intentions on more than one occasion, and not only when defeat seemed imminent. While General Mola, for example, affirmed, "A war of this nature must end in domination by the victor and absolute, total extermination of the loser," President Azaña declared during the early months of the war, "No policy can be based on a decision to exterminate the adversary... blood unjustly shed by hatred, with the intent to exterminate, is reborn and bears fruit that is cursed, not only for those who have caused blood to be shed, but for the entire nation that has absorbed it."

But in practice, there was a striking similarity between

the actions of the two sides. The Nationalists' efforts to exterminate the other side were directed more by the upper echelons, and were more militarized, although operations of "*limpieza*" (cleaning up) were often carried out by the Falange or by the Requetés in ways that evaded full control. The Republican's exterminating actions were more improvisational and decentralized, and often led by party militias or by spontaneous, autonomous repressive groups that were widely tolerated by helpless or conniving government authorities.

Someone has mercifully spread a handkerchief over one of the civilians killed in the shooting in Plaça de Catalunya in Barcelona on July 19, 1936. As soon as the military revolt began, it was clear that civilians would not be spared.
© Sergi i Octavi Centelles

No great differences existed between the killing methods of the two zones. In the early days of the war, uncertainty over the outcome of the conflict led men to kill immediately those who were seen as enemies. After the fronts had been established, this reaction developed into systematic manhunts, and to imprisonment in public or party jails (called *checas* in the Republican zone); nearly always prisoners left jail only to be executed in one of the frequent *sacas*, as the nightly removal of prisoners was called. The victims might or might not be condemned by military or popular courts, but they were led to the edge of a wood, to a cemetery wall or to the edge of a ditch they themselves had dug, and shot down. In Granada, that fate touched the poet, Federico García Lorca, who was guilty only of Republican sympathies and homosexuality. In August 1936, after a brief term in prison and no trial, he was shot in an olive grove.

But many did not even get as far as prison. The Falange squadrons or the groups of executioners with fanciful names – *brigada del amanecer* (dawn brigade), *coche fantasma* (ghost car) – operating in the Republican zone, led victims directly to the *paseo* (promenade), a tragically mocking expression meaning the "last trip." Behind both fronts, this often ended in a *cuneta* (ditch) at the side of the road.

Limpieza, sacas, paseo, cuneta: this vocabulary of terror and death common to the two combating sides characterized an identical phenomenon, generally called "repression." But these killings were not merely repres-

ATROCITIES ON BOTH SIDES

Above and beyond the opposing lines of propaganda accusing the adversary of the cruelest, most abject crimes, the horrors of the civil war were recorded in local news reports and in the memories of several witnesses. A reading of some of these accounts convinces us that the atrocities were not limited to either side. A Catalan peasant remembers: "A contractor from Barcelona who had fled to the town, was shot (by the militia) along with his sixteen-year-old son. But the son did not die. He was rescued and taken to the Tremp hospital. A few days later, though, they came to take him away from the hospital and this time, they killed him – by soaking him with gasoline and setting him on fire."
Later, the town would be occupied by Franco's army, leaving this memory of its passage: "They lined up everyone, except a girl, and shot them right off. I was so afraid that I didn't dare move, and stayed protected by the trees along the river. From that position I could see the girl was raped, just a few steps away from her mother's dead body. When they tired of that, they killed her." ■

– Gimeno, M. *Revolució al Pallars (1936–1939)*. Montserrat: Publicacions de l'Abadia de Montserrat, 1989. 30 & 71.

Testimony of the crimes is all the more chilling when given by the perpetrators themselves. Here is one such particularly tormented account, given by a young Galician Carlist: "I belonged to the repression brigades that began to operate in this city in August 1936, and you could soon see the results of our work. There is one scene I can never forget: the death of a young man by blows from a rifle butt. He wasn't over twenty years old. We had pulled him out of jail with the excuse of transferring him. His blood-soaked face, his cries – 'Please, kill me!' – I still see it and hear them even though more than forty years have passed. I wished I could have died too, that night of shame and disgrace. Sometimes, to console myself, I've read all the books about the same crimes committed by the other side. I know by heart the massacre of Paracuellos, the slaughter of Albacete, the torturing in Madrid's and Catalunya's *checas*, the shooting of religious. It has done me no good." ■

– Fernandez, C. *El Alzamiento en Galicia: Datos para una historia de la guerra civil.* La Coruna, 1982. 376.

sive actions meant to punish or prevent hostile acts, but really a bloody purge of all potential enemies, who were often picked out on the basis of their social standing. During the first days following the military coup, in zones falling under the control of one side or the other, there was a rabid search for the signs of identity that might mark the enemy. Those were the days in which a tie betraying bourgeois origins, or overalls betraying the factory worker, could cost a person his life. But it was political and union membership, above all, that determined whether one would live or die.

In the Nationalist zone, mainly on the basis of archives confiscated from various organizations, black lists were compiled naming members of parties and labor unions tied to the Popular Front, Masons, public officials, local administrators, and schoolteachers of Republican sympathies. In the Republican zone, as well, it was often sufficient to have belonged to one of the parties of the Right or Center or, as we have seen, to be a member of the clergy or any Catholic organization, to lose one's life.

Moderate positions, limited involvement, even distance in time from one's political engagement, were no guarantee of safety. For instance, a number of people,

The tragedy of the purge carried out by both sides was fed by the propaganda machine; each side accused the other of the most horrendous crimes. This image was disseminated by an Italian agency with the following caption: "In Barcelona, in Madrid, the shadiest figures of Spanish communism have taken command, and massacres and mass shootings are spectacles inebriating the red beasts. These are the bodies of young Spaniards killed at Irún."
© Publifoto

A *group of prisoners behind the Nationalist lines. Wrote Jay Allen of* The Chicago Tribune, *from Badajoz, three days after the Nationalists entered the city: "They were young, almost all of them peasants... at four in the morning they took them to the Plaza de Toros, where the machine gun was awaiting them. They say that the day after, the blood at the side of the street was palm deep. I don't doubt it: 1,800 were shot down in the space of twelve hours."*
© Publifoto

especially among the elderly, were victims of the Republican purge only because they had militated in the Unión Patriótica, a pseudo-party made up of notables, improvised by the dictator, Primo de Rivera, between 1924 and 1929. On the other side, especially after the war was over, numerous professional notables (vaguely progressive intellectuals, people of liberal sympathies, or merely supporters of regional autonomies), though convinced they were safe because of the small measure of their responsibilities, were led, still incredulous, to the execution platoon by the Francoist victors. One such person was the Andalusian regionalist, Blas Infante; another, remembered by Pierre Vilar, was the Catalan writer, Carles Rahola, whom one could hardly call a "Red." Nevertheless, he was executed at Gerona immediately after the war.

The purging function of the killings that happened behind both fronts shows up more clearly on the Nationalists' side precisely because one can verify the progression and uniformity of their conduct during and after the war. Indeed, after the conflict ended, the same elimination effort went on as before, with the same criteria, without pause; it merely became characterized by greater judicial formality. And it continued for years (the last death sentence was carried out in 1953, fourteen years after the end of the war), during which prisoners were submitted to the *garrote vil* (an atrocious form of torture) or shot. According to Francoist historians, the dead numbered 28,000; according to the opposition, they numbered 150,000.

At the same time, repression in the Republican zone, too, was also meant as a purge. All the more so in that it was often carried out not by the public authorities (who tended mostly to punish acts of concrete hostility toward the Republic, following on summary accusation by popular courts of justice), but by party militias, local revolutionary committees and spontaneous "executioners," the so-called "*incontrolados*" who operated at the edge or outside of political and union organizations.

Nor was there a lack of common criminal acts – armed robberies, thefts – committed by these popular "executioners"; they were more or less closely linked to the FAI and to the CNT, given the traditional concomitance between anarchist militancy and common criminality. But the criminal traits of the *incontrolados*' actions did not change the political nature of these actions: that is, the purging function common to the summary justice practiced by other militia committees.

The Catholic writer Georges Bernanos, who was in Spain from 1934 to 1936, recorded the fierce purge perpetuated by the Francoists on the island of Majorca in Les grands cimetiéres sous la lune, *published in 1938.*

State Massacres...

Soon, in the Nationalist Zone, and later, in the Republican, the purging action of repression was almost completely controlled by the State. But we cannot say it was any the less horrible, for that. The War Councils in the

BERNANOS AND THE PURGES

The French Catholic novelist, Georges Bernanos, who lived through the experience of the civil war on the island of Majorca, has left chilling testimony of the merciless purges committed by the Nationalists, led by so-called Count Rossi, the Italian Fascist, Arconovaldo Bonaccorsi, who had taken command of the island. Bernanos's book, *Les grands cimetiéres sous la lune*, had a strong impact on world opinion, partly because its author was a traditionalist Catholic who would have been expected to militate in favor of the other side. Here is his account of the summary executions.

"The first phase of the purge lasted four months, during which the foreigner, the one mainly responsible for these massacres, was never absent from the place of honor in all the religious manifestations... Until December, the ditches around the cemeteries on the island produced their funereal crops of evil-minded persons. Workers and peasants, but also bourgeois, pharmacists, notary publics...

"Once the summary purge had nearly burned itself out, it was necessary to see to the prisons. They were full, just think! And the concentration camps were full too. And barges no longer in use were full, their sinister decks kept under surveillance night and day; in an excess of precaution, after night fell the gloomy paintbrush of a searchlight passed back and forth over them. Oh, I saw it from bed! Then began the second phase, the prison purge. In fact, a great number of these suspects, men and women, could not be touched by martial law, since they had committed not even the most insignificant material misdemeanor subject to condemnation by a war council. So they began to release them in groups, according to their place of origin. Half way along, they emptied the load into the ditch." ■

– translated from Bernanos, G. *I grandi cimiteri sotto la luna*. Milan: Mondadori, 1992. 131–132.

***T**he bombardment of Guérnica took place on Monday afternoon, April 26, 1937, with successive waves of Junkers J–52s and Heinkel 111s of the Condor Legion. The only target that might have held any military interest, the bridge over the Mundaca, remained intact. 1,500 dead were counted, and about 1,000 wounded.*
© L'Illustration/Sygma/T

Nationalist zone issued whole series of death sentences. While a few generic adversaries might hope to receive a prison sentence, there was no escape for those who had actively opposed the coup; they were judged to be guilty of "military rebellion" (!) – a true judicial monstrosity, as such judgments were admitted to be much later, by Serrano Suñer (Franco's brother-in-law) himself.

The so-called Popular Tribunals were no less hasty. Created with the actual purpose of putting a stop to summary justice as carried out by political parties and other groups, in many cases they were compelled to satisfy these groups' thirst for vengeance. Composed mostly of members of political and union organizations, they were not much different from the corresponding military tribunals on the other side, in their methods or in the time it took them to issue death sentences.

At any rate, not even an appearance of justice characterized the two great mass slaughterings perpetrated by the opposing powers. The first was performed in August 1936 by the Nationalists, in the *Plaza de Toros* of Badajoz. There, all the "Reds" that it had been possible to find had been rounded up, together with the militiamen who had strenuously defended the city. 3,000, perhaps 4,000 men (here, too, it is difficult to disentangle true testimony from propaganda) were shot down by machine guns. Colonel Yagüe, who had given the order to shoot, justified himself by saying that he could not leave so many enemies at his back.

The second massacre occurred in the Republican zone, and was perhaps even crueler, in its premeditation and duration in time. After early November 1936, many convoys carrying loads of political prisoners were sent out several times from Madrid, which was under siege; the men were supposed to be transferred to other jails, so that they would not be liberated if the city fell. But in reality, the trucks onto which they had been squeezed together were driven to Paracuellos del Jarama and other nearby towns. There, the prisoners were made to get out, shot down with automatic weapons and then buried in a dry canal and other ditches. At the end of the war, more than 2,000 bodies were exhumed from these common graves.

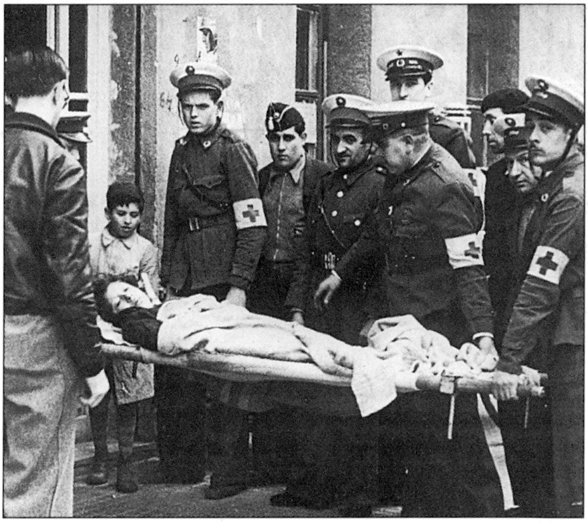

Response to the bombings (here, in Barcelona, in March of 1937) was often an assault on prisons, and reprisal against prisoners, who in such cases became true scapegoats.
© Publifoto.

The bombing of Guérnica belongs to this category of massacre. Indeed, although it was presented as a war operation, its traits marked it as a terrorist, punitive action. It was an act intending to exterminate and destroy the center of a city; an act wholly obedient to the logic of civil war in that it deliberately went beyond a military context in order to wage direct aggression against civilians.

This episode was part of the strategy carried out in April 1937 by the Nationalist army with the aim of conquering the Basque country. But Guérnica had no strategic relevance. It had no military installations, nor war industries. Therefore it had no defense against air raids. Instead, with its ancient oak tree beneath which Spanish sovereigns once promised to respect the privileges of those populaces, it was the symbolic heart of Basque independence. The nature of the attack – the incendiary bombs that went on in waves for a whole afternoon, the machine-gun attacks against the populace – leaves no doubt that the air raid's objectives were the city itself, and its inhabitants. The complete destruction of Guérnica and the more than 1,000 victims, clearly testified to this fact.

A foreshadowing of World War II, it was such an extra-

THE BOMBING OF GUERNICA

What really happened in Guérnica on the afternoon of April 26, 1937? According to an interview given by General Franco the following July to a correspondent from the *Liverpool Daily Post*, it had been the "reds" who had blown the town up with dynamite and set it on fire, as they had done at Irún, Durango, Amerobieta and other towns of the Basque country. This was a colossal lie, stubbornly repeated for years by Francoist propaganda, and adamantly denied not only by the opposing side, but also by historians. Finally in 1971, Colonel Martínez Bande, director of the Military History service at the Spanish Defense Ministry during the last years of the dictatorship, published a book giving an absolutely undeniable technical report of the event. Between 4:15 P.M. and 7:30 P. M. that day, successive waves of Heinkel and Junkers aircraft from the Condor Legion, after taking off from the Vitoria airport, struck the city with explosive and incendiary bombs, repeatedly machine-gunning the civilian population. The ancient urban center was almost completely destroyed. Once we have established these facts, two questions remain open: was the city a military objective, or was this a deliberate terrorist bombing? And was the operation directly ordered by Franco? In terms of the first point, the operation's methods seem to leave no doubt that the targets were the residential area and the populace, considering that the Basque army contingent that had settled on the outskirts remained unharmed by the attack, and the bridge and a pistol factory – other objectives indicated by Francoist historians – remained intact. Regarding the second point, it is impossible to reach a definite verdict on the basis of documents available.

While it is true that Franco was in no position to publicly dissociate himself from a German initiative, and that therefore his not having done so does not prove his responsibility, there is no proof of his having made even the most timid protest in diplomatic documents; nor is there any concrete evidence of other autonomous initiatives on the part of the German air force in Spain. ■

ordinarily serious act that it awakened indignation throughout the world. For a long time, Franco denied his responsibility, accusing the Republicans themselves of destroying the city for propaganda purposes! Later, when it could no longer be denied the Condor Legion had been responsible for the bombing, the Nationalists maintained that it had acted without the Spanish command's knowledge. But this hypothesis was highly improbable, since all the German armed forces operating in Spain were allowed to go into action only upon receiving orders from Franco.

Pablo Picasso's famous painting inspired by the bombing represents not only the horror, but also the fear awakened by Guérnica. What fate was approaching for the peoples of the world, in the face of governments unafraid to use such terrible instruments of massacre?

In this Republican poster, the angel of peace is a Nazi skeleton launching bombs from the sky. The Germans from the Condor Legion that Goring sent to Spain numbered 4,000; in the theater of Spain's civil war, they experimented with the bombing techniques widely adopted in the Second World War.

...And Popular Massacres

In the face of these cold, lucid massacres committed by the public powers on the basis of cost-and-profit calculations, in the face of thousands of nightly executions usually committed "for the sake of an idea" rather than to punish crimes, the fierce popular violence that sometimes exploded in response seems terrible, but human and instinctive. The "Fascists" of Ronda who were thrown off a cliff, or those of Ciudad Real cast into the well of a mine, or of Santander, pushed off the shoal of Cabo Mayor, certainly did suffer a horrible death. But the gesture of killing here seems full of passion, of rancor, of hatred or punitive terror pervaded by an ancient culture that threw criminals and the damned into hell. Around those deaths, there is not the silence that surrounded the executions. There is the cry of furor, blind, uncivil and extremely human, that precedes a futile revenge for offenses suffered. A cry breaking out at moments of helpless suffering, at moments when heaven betrays.

Left, loading of a Condor Legion Heinkel 111, ready for takeoff.
© Publifoto

The bombing of civilian populations was the most frequent type of bombing at the time. The response to that scourge was often proud and courageous. Such was the Madrileños' response. Destruction and slaughter did not bend their will to resist. But they often resorted to a desperate kind of violence, futile in its vindictiveness: an immediate, bloody reprisal against imprisoned men.

As early as August 1936, the first air raid on the capital unleashed an assault against prisoners in the jail of Modello: 30 of the best-known men of the Right, imprisoned there, were shot by an execution platoon. The same happened in Bilbao in January 1937, when a rabid crowd assaulted the prison after an attack by German bomber planes. With help from the very soldiers called in to turn it back, the crowd massacred about 200 prisoners. Naval bombings produced the same effects: at the end of October 1936, for example, the raid by a Nationalist battle cruiser in the bay of Roses provoked the extermination of prisoners in much of Catalunya.

***A** mother peers at the sky as the siren announces a raid by Nazi aviation.*
© Publifoto

The same thing happened in the Nationalist zone. Huesca, Valladolid, Granada, La Línea are only some of the localities where such scenes took place. There, as later occurred in the Republican zone as well, reprisal was ritualized. Execution by gunshot systematically followed every air raid. Shootings became almost a bureaucratic task. In reporting an air attack that had struck the city, Dionisio Ridruejo, one of the leaders of the Falange in Segovia, described reprisal against the prisoners as an "inevitable consequence" of that raid.

In this case, too, the normalization of reprisal involved

a sort of expropriation of popular revenge. But such revenge did break out again from time to time, especially when news spread of a military revolt, the loss of a city, or the death of a fellow townsman or political leader. That was what happened, for example, at Tafalla, in Navarra, after the funeral of a Requeté lieutenant killed

Grief after the bombardment of Lérida, in November 1937.
© Sergi i Octavi Centelles

BOMBED CITIES

We are perhaps too used to the catastrophic images of the Second World War to understand what a traumatic novelty the bombardments were for the Spanish population. Pablo Neruda, the Chilean poet who served as his country's ambassador to Spain, recounts and explains that horror, noting what a profound effect it had on his own way of being a poet.

I'm Explaining a Few Things
You are going to ask: and where
are the lilacs?
and the poppy-petalled
metaphysics?
and the rain repeatedly spattering
its words and drilling them full
of apertures and birds?
I'll tell you all the news.
I lived in a suburb,
a suburb of Madrid, with bells,
and clocks and trees.
From there you could look out
over Castille's dry face:
a leather ocean.
My house was called
the house of flowers, because in
every cranny
geraniums burst...
And one morning all that was
burning,
one morning the bonfires
leapt out of the earth
devouring human beings –
and from then on fire,
gunpowder from then on,
and from then on blood.
Bandits with planes and Moors,
bandits with finger-rings and
duchesses,
bandits with black friars
spattering blessings
came through the sky to kill
children
and the blood of children ran
through the streets
without fuss, like children's blood.
And you will ask: why doesn't his
poetry
speak of dreams and leaves
and the great volcanoes of his
native land?
Come and see the blood in the
streets...■

– Neruda, P. *Selected Poems.* Boston: Houghton Mifflin, 1990. 150–155.

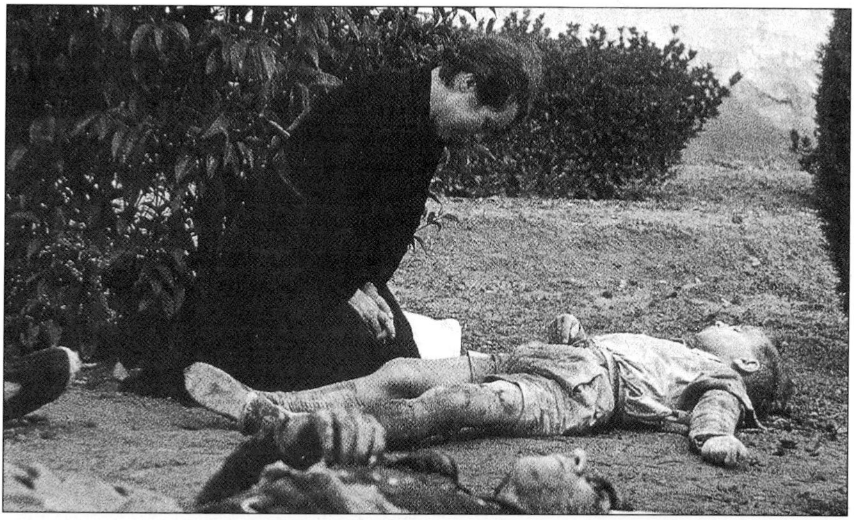

at the front. All of 59 prisoners were immolated to his memory. The same fate was suffered by 18 prisoners at Igualada, in Catalunya, when the rumor spread that Joaquín Maurín, one of the POUM leaders, had been shot by the Nationalists. (Later, the rumor turned out to be false.)

These were mainly vindictive acts but basically, they also were intended as a purge. They were dominated by an eagerness to free the community from a hidden enemy by way of violence against a known or presumed enemy. This was the "fifth-column effect" – an expression destined to become internationally famous; an

MARITAIN: THE CONTRADICTIONS OF A HOLY WAR

In an article entitled "De la guerre sainte" which appeared in *Nouvelle Revue Franéaise*, in July 1937, Jacques Maritain denounced the horrors of civil war, unmasking the contradictions implicit in the ethical and spiritual motivations of both sides in combat: "It is a horrible sacrilege to massacre priests – even though they might be 'Fascists,' they are still ministers of Christ – out of spite for religion; and it is no less horrible a sacrilege to massacre the poor – even though they might be 'Marxists,' they are the people of Christ – in the name of religion. It is clearly a sacrilege to burn churches and holy images, sometimes in blind fury, and sometimes, as in Barcelona, with a cold anarchist method and beastly schematization; and it is again, a sacrilege – in the form of religion – to deck out Muslim soldiers with images of the Sacred Heart so they will kill the sons of Christians in a holy manner, and pretend to enroll God in the passions of a struggle in which the adversary is considered to be unworthy of any respect or pity. It is a sacrilege to profane holy places and the Holy Sacrament, to persecute everything consecrated to God, to dishonor and torture religious women, exhume cadavers and abandon them to ridicule, as we have seen done in the dark days following the explosion of the war; and it is a sacrilege to shoot, as in Badajoz, hundreds of men in order to celebrate the day of the Assumption, or to annihilate with bombs, as in Durango – since holy war hates believers who do not serve it more ardently than nonbelievers do – the churches and the people filling them, and the priests celebrating the mysteries; or, as in Guérnica, an entire town, with its churches and tabernacles, cutting down poor fleeing people with machine guns." ■

In the atmosphere of civil war, a closed fist might signify a life saved, as in the case of these Augustinian nuns forced to fraternize with a group of militia.
© Publifoto

effect condensing the anguished fear of an unknown threat and an unrecognizable enemy. Such an effect was produced by General Mola's intimidating declarations that a fifth column hiding in the city was awaiting the right moment to join the four columns then assaulting Madrid. In such situations, invisible danger, feared betrayal, and fear of ambush awaken a nervous punitive violence. A terrible vicious cycle is set in motion: whoever is a suspect hides, and whoever hides is a conspirator, and is to be eliminated.

In such a context, one can better understand how such a particular ferocity against priests could break out: they were so easily identifiable. A liberating wave of violence was unleashed on them; especially when, having abandoned their clerical garb in order to flee their persecutors, they were made out just the same because of their poorly-hidden tonsures, or their daily habits. But it was not only their recognizable nature that drew such violence, and particularized it. This violence sometimes took on archaic forms; it almost seemed to repeat forms that had already appeared in the old religious wars; at any rate, it was pervaded with religious culture, comprising both the idea of retaliation with the pains of hell, and a blasphemous, sacrilegious protest.

The widespread anticlericalism in the Republican zone was often expressed in the macabre act of exhuming the cadavers of the religious. Only in the Basque region was the church safe from persecution: both because of greater control by Republican authorities (who were mostly Catholic), and because of the local Church's traditional support for Basque autonomy.

Mutilation, torture, blinding, atrocious wounding, the dragging of cadavers, stations of martyrdom re-evoking scenes of the Passion: these were the sufferings that many Catholics underwent, according to the diocesan accounts of martyrs and the many canonization causes opened after the war. And although the phenomenon was certainly exaggerated for the purposes of propaganda, the testimony is too convincing and widespread to deny the seed of truth in these accounts. Such a truth acquires greater credibility in the context of a whole series of widely-documented, exasperated,

Relics and liturgical objects are prepared for the bonfire. In response to accusations by many Catholic intellectuals – from the Frenchman, Maritain, to the Italian, Sturzo – Cardinal Goma, urged by Franco, issued the "Collective letter from the Spanish Episcopate" to bishops all over the world. Promulgated on July 1, 1937, the letter was signed by 48 Spanish bishops. It was not signed by the bishops of Tarragona or Vitoria.
© Publifoto

violent acts damaging holy images. Body parts of the statues and images were amputated, including their sexual organs; eyes were pierced; degrading, mocking gestures were made. Even more important, cemeteries and tombs conserving the bodies of priests and nuns were violated.

This was a widespread phenomenon, photographically documented and widely distributed throughout the Republican zone. Ancient and more recent cadavers of Catholics were dug up from cemeteries, and from tombs in the floors of churches, and displayed to the public in various stages of decomposition. The dried mummies of nuns or priests were exhibited as if they were macabre scarecrows or grotesque sentinels. Skeletons were often dismembered, skulls and other bones mixed together and scattered about.

The violation of dead bodies was a point of encounter and mediation in a flux of violence that passed from human beings to images, and vice versa. If people could not lash out at the living, they found its best substitution in motionless, rotten cadavers. At the same time that wooden images were personified, dead bodies were transformed into objects and shown in all their impotence and fragility. So easily could they be dismembered; so easily could they be violated and thrown away.

Both religious and social motivations influenced all

acts of anticlerical violence, more intimately than just what the will to punish the complicity between the clergy and men of power, might seem to suggest. As André Gide wrote, in order to emancipate themselves socially, the popular masses of Spain also had to "break the shell" of their religion. And they did so in this most terrible form, because there was a patrimony of culture, values, and persecutory and purging needs, shared by that Church – which was, after all, the Church of the Inquisition, the Church most infamous for its persecution of heretics – and its enemies. This shared patrimony was expressed in symmetrical acts of violence that formed an almost uninterrupted chain stretching from ancient to modern times.

THE EXHIBITION OF CADAVERS

From initially being an iconoclastic, sacrilegious act, the exhibition of exhumed cadavers often became a macabre carnival show. This is how María Ochoa, who was thirteen at the time, remembers what happened in Barcelona; her testimony is reported by the English historian, Ronald Fraser: "They dug up the nun's corpses, too, and displayed the skeletons and mummies. I found that quite amusing; so did all the kids. When we got bored looking at the same ones in my neighborhood, we'd go to another *barrio* to see the ones they'd dug up there... We kids would make comments about the different corpses – how this one was well-preserved, and that one decomposed, this one older; we got a lot of amusement out of it all..." ■

– Fraser, R. *Blood of Spain: An Oral History of the Spanish Civil War.* New York: Pantheon, 1979. 152.

Chapter 6

ROADS TO DEFEAT AND VICTORY

IN THE SUMMER OF 1938 THE OUTCOME OF THE WAR BECOMES CLEAR. WHILE FRANCO'S *RECONQUISTA* ADVANCES FROM CITY TO CITY, THE REPUBLIC AND THE NEGRÍN GOVERNMENT AGONIZE. BUT WAS DEFEAT REALLY INEVITABLE?

One year after the Negrín government had been formed, the defeat of the Republic appeared more and more probable. The international scene, which has already been indicated as a cause, was also a sign of such a development. The side emerging from the battlefields as loser, also lost the capacity to find new alliances; old friendships grew cold, while the victors' friends increased in number. But it was above all within the confines of the peninsula that the reasons for the imminent defeat were to be found.

The remains of the Republican army cross the French border. The defeat of the Republic was caused not so much by the inferiority of means available, but by the better military training of the Francoist soldiers and officers. The Republican army never succeeded in carrying out an offensive strike capable of taking the initiative in the war.
© Publifoto

Questions about Defeat

Did the frustration of revolutionary ambitions, of the "we want it all right now" line that many had thought feasible, dishearten many combatants of Republican Spain? Is this the key to the defeat of the Republic, as has been suggested?

Although the change in direction that occurred in May of 1937 could not help but dampen the enthusiasm of many revolutionary militants, it is highly improbable that the latter lost all motive for defending the Republic. At least one motive remained, and it was a very strong one. What was to be expected from the enemy's victory? Was not the regime that the enemy offered much worse than the "democratic bourgeois" Republic? And those who had been most visible – through their expropriations, their collectivizations, and their antifascist purges – wondered what treatment they could expect from the winners of the conflict. These were very good reasons for keeping up a tenacious resistance, in spite of disappointments suffered. And it was no coincidence that the CNT and the FAI, in spite of dissension and grumbling within their ranks, stood strong almost until the end, following the all-out defense policy advocated by the Negrín government.

Rather than the political militants, it was the populace at large that noticeably weakened in their will to resist. The masses had less to fear from defeat; their ideas were less clear, their convictions less strong. The people had joined in the fight because they had been called to arms; they were more and more exhausted by a long-lasting conflict, disappointed by military setbacks, disillusioned now that they were not on the winning side. The mythical "resistance of the Spanish people" more and more only involved certain active minorities. Their capacity for dragging along the rest of the populace, that fluid mass tending to inertia whose movements were decisive for victory, inevitably waned with the passing of time. But this alone does not explain the defeat of the Republic.

***A** poster put out by the metal-workers' union of the FAI-CNT. In the last months of the war, while military defeats were undermining civilian morale, the unions and the people most committed to the Republic gathered around Negrín, who was an advocate of all-out resistance.*

Independent of hindsight, let us make an effort to understand what prospects were opening up for the new Republican government, after the middle of May 1937. It had only one aim: to wage war and win. It was formed with that intent; and to those who criticized him for one reason or another, Negrín often responded peremptorily: "I make war." Without a doubt, that was to be the fundamental aim now; and at that date, it was still possible to achieve it. The effort failed for a series of reasons, none of which, alone, prefigured the inevitability of defeat.

A war is lost, first of all, on the battlefield; and the Spanish war was no exception. As we have seen, the Republic was unable to win any but a few defensive battles, both before and after the Negrín government. The reason for this is the most obvious one imaginable: the adversary, the Nationalists, were militarily superior.

What gave rise to this superiority? The first thing to consider is the matter of armaments. Despite what many supporters of the Republic have claimed, this was not the decisive factor. Although the flow of Soviet aid was less dependable, it was on the whole equivalent to aid received by the Nationalists from the Axis powers, and it continued until the end of the war. As late as the middle of January 1939, when the situation could be considered desperate, a vast quantity of armaments arrived from the Soviet Union: 400 aircraft, 400,000 rifles, 10,000 machine guns (though a considerable part was blocked at the French border).

The problem, instead, touched on the effective use of those arms. Not only in the restricted sense of their use in battle, but also in the sense of logistics (in their correct and timely use where necessary) and in the sense of strategy (in the choice, made as rapidly as possible, of where to employ arms, and to what end). This brings us to consider two fundamental, and connected, matters: the capacity for military leadership, and the capacity for political leadership in the war. Let us consider these matters in what was the Republic's last great chance: the battle of the Ebro.

Thrown back in the battle for Madrid, after having failed in all successive attempts to get around the capital (in particular, via the Guadalajara road), Franco moves the war northward: first by conquering the Basque country, then by advancing toward the Mediterranean, thus cutting in two the Republican territory; and finally, by attacking Catalunya.

Colonel Modesto's troops cross the Ebro on July 26, 1938, to launch the last and most famous Republican offensive of the civil war. In the course of a week, the army filled up the inlet formed by the Ebro River between Fayon and Certa, consolidating a bridgehead in the Gandesa hills, in order to resist the furious Francoist counteroffensive.

The Battle of the Ebro

There was no battle that the Republican side faced in more favorable conditions than that of the Ebro. In July 1938, the Negrín government had reached the apex of its authority. No autonomous power had remained standing in the Republican zone: the fall of the North saw the disappearance of the Basque autonomous government, the Santander Junta and the Sovereign Committee of Asturias; the Aragon Council had been dissolved; the Catalan government had been almost completely deprived of power. Political dissidence had been quelled and cast aside: Caballero, who had tried to gain vindication through the labor union, once again found himself in a minority position; the anarchist organizations created no further problems (a member of the CNT had even re-entered the government), worn down as they were by an irreversible internal crisis; even Prieto's group and the defeatists had been marginalized.

In several sectors, a great deal of discontent was created by the fact that the Communists, of whom Negrín was considered to be the ideological offspring, progressively came to occupy most of the key posts in the administration and the army. This policy was openly followed by the International – and by Togliatti, its main executor in

Spain – especially because the Communists were the most reliable interpreters of the policy of all-out defense, and advocated subordination of any other objectives to the war effort. But it was also a practice giving rise to accusations that Moscow was subjecting Spain to its ends (consider the fact that most of the gold of the Bank of Spain had ended up in the Soviet Union); and it favored the intentions of those who advocated the possibility of reaching a peace agreement with Franco for the sake of anti-Communism. Nevertheless, on the eve of the Ebro maneuvers, Negrín still held the reins of power firmly in his hands.

The international panorama was certainly not favorable. Franco's victories strengthened the convictions of those within democratic countries who were hostile to the Republican government. In France, Blum was forced to abandon the government; first it was left in the hands of the radical Chautemps and then, after Blum's very brief return, to Daladier; they were both more preoccupied than he had been with the need to avoid any risk of war, and were therefore more accommodating in the face of Italo-German aggression. In England, Eden, the foreign minister, who wanted to stand firm toward the Fascist powers, was replaced by Lord Halifax, who was quite willing to make an agreement to the detriment of the Spanish Republic. What followed was the Anglo-Italian pact of April 1938, ratifying Britain's agreement to the presence of Italian troops in Spain, in exchange for Mussolini's promise to abandon the Iberian territory once the war was over.

"Non-intervention," therefore, continued to be the "farce" that it is now recognized as. And the Nationalists exploited the situation. From the sea or by way of Portugal, they continued receiving a regular flow of aid and arms from the Italians and the Germans, not to mention fuel provided by American oil

During the civil war, the Soviet aircraft Polikarpov, nicknamed "rata" (mouse) was the most widespread fighter in the heterogeneous Republican airforce. Despite its constant inferiority to the Nationalist airforce, in the Ebro battle the Republican airforce managed to protect the infantry so that it could cross the river.
© Publifoto

companies. Aid to the Republic was more discontinuous, because Italian, German and Nationalist warships sank with impunity all ships in the Mediterranean that were heading for Republican ports. The USSR was forced to abandon the Mediterranean route between Murmansk and Bordeaux. From that city, transport lines had to arrive in Spain overland, crossing the French border.

General Vincente Rojo (center) with Juan Negrín (left). The military objective of the Ebro battle, planned by Rojo (one of the few talented Republican officers), was to divert the Francoists from their advance on Valencia. The political objective was to bring relief and restore credibility to the Negrín government, in the hopes of rallying support for the Republic from France and England, who were facing Hitler's expansionism.

But in spite of several interruptions (after all, the French had been the ones to propose "non-intervention" in the first place, so they were expected to try to make it work), transport along that route turned out to flow fairly smoothly, too. Not only did Blum's government leave a passage open, but successive governments did so as well. Therefore, at the moment of the Ebro offensive, the Republican army was extremely well-equipped, except for its insufficient air protection.

On the dawn of July 26, Colonel Yagüe, who had settled in with his Moroccan troops along the great arm formed by the Ebro River between Fayón and Certa, must have been enormously surprised to notice that most of a large Republican army had crossed the river during the night, on board rafts, while military engineers were hurriedly laying down bridges to allow the passage of tanks, artillery and motorized convoys. The surprise was not simply about the Republic's capacity to carry out such an enormous, silent crossing, but also about the fact that it was still capable of performing such an imposing military effort. Quickly it was necessary to acknowledge that this was not one of the usual actions of disturbance. Within four days an army of 250,000 well-armed men, commanded by General Hernandez Sarabia and, in the two main sectors, by Colonels Perea and Modesto, succeeded in taking over the entire bay area delineated by the river, establishing itself along a front focalized around the town of Gandesa: this in spite of furious bombardment from enemy aviation.

Surprise ran not only through Franco's army, but also throughout the governments of Europe. This was Negrín's main objective – perhaps the only one. The Spanish dilemma, which had seemed on the way to a rapid solution, opened up again. Negrín had first appeared conciliatory, in his proposal of a thirteen-point peace plan; his conditions were very reasonable, but they only served to show his good will in the face of Franco's intransigence (Franco now being sure of victory). Now the Ebro offensive showed the democratic powers that Republican Spain could resist and deserved aid, in order to create a common front against Fascist aggression (indeed, the Anschluss, the annexation of Austria to the German Reich, had occurred in March; and Germany was now threatening Czechoslovakia).

But beyond such considerations, did the Ebro offensive not have more concrete war objectives? The plan made by Rojo, its strategist (though it was Negrín who chose the

"Resist! Resist!" says Stalin, sitting on Negrín's shoulders, in this Nationalist cartoon that lampoons the Republic and its dependence on Soviet aid.

GOLD FROM THE BANK OF SPAIN

Soviet aid to the Spanish Republic was not without conditions, even in purely economic terms. In order to guarantee payment both to the Soviet Union and to third-party suppliers, Largo Caballero's government had to transfer most of the Bank of Spain's gold reserves to Russia. (Part of the gold reached France, and was given back to Franco after the war.) The Republicans had also wanted to protect that vast deposit from being confiscated by Franco, but their decision was nevertheless disastrous to their "image." What better argument could there be for enemy propaganda than the abandonment of the nation's wealth to a foreign power, in apparently total subjection to Communism? From then on, the black legend of the "gold of Moscow" became one of the themes of Nationalist propaganda for the entire duration of the regime. The cargo of gold, which totalled 500 tons and was contained in about 8,000 chests, was loaded on board four Soviet ships in the port of Cartagena. They sailed for Odessa on October 25, 1936. With successive orders during the course of the war, the deposit shrank, until it dwindled down to nothing. Indeed, the last arms supplies were conceded by the Soviet Union on credit.
But overall, that country proved to be much less generous than the Fascist powers, which gave Franco massive aid on credit. ■

plan among various alternatives) expressed the intention of preventing the Nationalist army from continuing its advance on Valencia, which Franco had been accomplishing slowly but unceasingly. In preventing the advance, the Republican forces made it possible for the army of the Center, commanded by Miaja, to reorganize and then carry out an offensive against Estremadura (an action that had been envisioned so often before). In this way, the Nationalist territory would be broken in two, opening Andalusia to invasion.

But only the first part of the plan was carried out. Franco did abandon the Valencian front, and led the best elements of his forces to converge on the Ebro inlet. Thus began a bloody battle, a senseless one from a military point of view. Except for the massive use of air bombings, it was wholly similar to battles fought in World War I on the western front: frenetically insistent frontal attacks by the infantry, alternating between small attacks and retreats, with enormous losses on both sides. After three and a half months, the battle ended with the retreat of the Republican army to its initial position, on the other side of the river.

Franco was criticized for his war conduct in these circumstances by many of his allies. Even some elements in his army criticized him, albeit timidly. He could very well have consolidated a bridgehead on the Gandesa front, and worked around the enemy positions, easily moving away into Catalunya. Instead, he preferred to engage himself in a war of attrition, with heavy losses, perhaps delaying his final victory. But as before, he stubbornly refused to concede even one victory to the enemy; with his refusal, he probably meant to inflict a heavy blow on the adversary's morale. If this was his aim, he certainly succeeded. The remaining part of Rojo's plan was not even partially fulfilled. The army of the Center, in fact, was unable to carry out any operation in direct support of the Ebro army, while in Estremadura, Miaja underwent Queipo de Llano's attacks, rather than weakening the enemy with his offensive.

During the Ebro battle the border was closed a number of times, which prevented the Republican armies from receiving a sufficient flow of armaments. But the problem of military equipment was not the fundamental one for the Republic. It is not unusual to hear of armies that are infe-

rior in number and armaments, and win battles all the same – and sometimes even wars. The problem reflected the quality of the Republic's armed forces, and their leadership. As we have seen, there was a great lack of intermediate commanding hierarchy; and this gap could certainly not be filled by accelerated courses in the Popular War Schools, especially for battalion commanders, or chiefs of staff. In addition, the high command was mediocre and irresolute, with the possible exception of Rojo (but at the start of the war, he had been a simple major; only with the advent of Negrín's government did he assume strategic leadership).

It is not that Franco was a military genius. His strategic conduct has been judged excessively prudent, slow and conservative. Although the superiority of his means would have allowed it, he was never capable of leading a rapid, routing, definitive campaign against the enemy (or perhaps he did not want to, for political reasons). But he was favored by an army gifted with expert commanders; an army able to finely train those new troop officers, the *alféreces provisionales* (provisional second lieutenants), that became the backbone of his army. Thanks to them, without a doubt, the war waged by the military won out over the war waged by the people.

The Ebro battle demonstrated Franco's determination not to lose a single battle. On November 15, 1938, after nearly four months of hard, trench-to-trench combat, the last Republican brigade crossed back over the Ebro. Above, the soldiers of the agonized Republican army retreat toward the French border.
Left, a Nationalist flag is raised on a position taken from the Republicans.
© 2 Publifoto

From Spanish War to World War

With the passing of time, the Spanish Civil War definitely lost its national character. In Spain, people were fighting against the "Reds" and against the Fascists. On one side there was Soviet Russia, and on the other, Nazi Germany and Fascist Italy. If these powers withdrew their arms, the war would disappear: the Spanish skies would be empty. At any rate, that was how the inhabitants of democratic countries saw the events. Spain was only one of the fracture points in a precariously-balanced world peace.

That is why at the end of September 1938, while the Ebro battle was being waged, the war's outcome could be determined in Munich. The heads of four European powers hastened there, to a conference called to resolve the question of Czechoslovakia, which was about to be invaded by the Germans. In the days preceding the conference, Negrín had made use of all his diplomatic resources, hoping to convince the French government of the need to resist against Germany, whose aggressiveness, both in Spain and Czechoslovakia, was encouraged by the accommodating attitude of the democratic powers. Negrín made his case by reminding the Western powers that, should the conflict become widespread, having a Fascist country on

In the face of Franco's advance, a group of civilians follows the retreat of Republicans trying to get away from the front. Many took refuge in Barcelona, which fell without the firing of a single shot in January 1939. Others formed long lines attempting to cross the French border.
© Publifoto

the southern border would be dangerous. Republican Spain could play an important part in the defense of all democratic countries.

For his part, Franco had hastened to assure France and England of his absolute neutrality in the eventuality of a European war. There was no need to do so. In Munich, as is well-known, a near-sighted desire for peace once more dominated the conduct of the French and English government leaders, who were encouraged to take this position by many sectors of public opinion in their countries. Thus the conference ended with the acceptance of Germany's occupation of the Sudetanland; later, when the Spanish war was over, Germany would invade the entire Czechoslovakian territory, with the acquiescence of the majority of powers.

With the sacrificing of Czechoslovakia, Republican Spain's few remaining hopes evaporated. But Czechoslovakia's redemption, too, might have brought about the same result; if the democratic powers in Munich had forced Hitler to give up the Sudetanland, they might have been willing to compensate him by giving up Spain. The only way of escape for the Republic, then, was war. So it was that the English ambassador in Spain, John Leche, defined Negrín in his dispatches as one of the principal enemies of peace in Europe.

Nevertheless, by the time the Munich conference was over, even Negrín had been won over to the idea of peace by compromise. With this aim, and under English pressure, in November he agreed to dissolve the International Brigades, as a sign of good will. But what motive did the Nationalists have for seeking compromise, in the face of a divided enemy who was discouraged and near collapse?

For some time now, many in the Republican zone had given up the war for lost. They were wondering how to get out of it with the least harm possible. Contrary to Negrín's and the Communists' line of resistance, they had begun to imagine alternate solutions that might spare further bloodshed. President Azaña stood out among this group.

Back from the Munich conference, the British Prime Minister, Neville Chamberlain, waves a copy of the pact made with Hitler, which he thought would bring peace. The pact marked the end of the last, tenuous hopes of the Spanish Republic.
© Publifoto

He stood on the sidelines of the conflict, growing gloomier and gloomier in his lucid pessimism. In fact, as early as May 1937, he had written a play, *La velia a Benicarlo,* which ended with the image of the Republican zone in ruins. But other moderate personalities as well, such as Martínez Barrio, Besteiro, Prieto, the representatives of the Catalan and Basque nationalist parties, and some of the military, began more and more openly to disagree with the government in charge, and tried to weave together alternatives in order to achieve peace as painlessly as possible.

THE FALL OF BARCELONA

General Rojo left detailed testimony of the collapse of the Catalan front. Here is his bitter comment on the failed defense of Barcelona:

"On January 26, Barcelona fell to the enemy. The feared event occurred like a natural phenomenon. Resistance was scarce, not to say null. The enemy succeeded in entering the city and was able to continue its movement westward with the same ease it had used in the days preceding... "One cannot help but note a tremendous contrast. The situation of Madrid in November 1936 was very similar to the one we have described in Barcelona. But what a different atmosphere! What enthusiasm then! What a feverish desire to fight, two years before, and what discouragement now! 48 hours before the enemy's entry, Barcelona was a dead city. It had been killed by the demoralization of those who fled to France, and those who remained in hiding, without even the courage to go out into the streets, or end those last hours of bitterness destined for the city. For this reason, it is no exaggeration to say that Barcelona was lost simply because there was no will to resist, either among the populace or among certain troops that had been contaminated by the atmosphere. Morale was crushed." ■

– Rojo, V. *¡Alerta los pueblos!* Barcelona: Ariel, 1974. 124–126.

The developments of the war rendered vain all those internal disputes, even while it continued to keep them alive. On Christmas Eve in 1938, Franco launched his attack on Catalunya, with an army of 250,000 men, about 1,000 artillery pieces and 500 aircraft. The offensive followed two lines of penetration: from the north, along the line of the Segre river, and from the south, in the area of Serós. The Republican army confronting Franco was almost as large, but was less well-armed and had only half the aircraft. The Republicans were not surprised: they had been aware of preparations for the attack, and had actually expected it to come sooner.

But troop morale was bad. And behind the lines, the populace was not at all ready to sustain a long siege. Once again, Rojo had planned a series of military operations to disperse the enemy forces: one in Andalusia, which was to include nothing less than a landing at Motril, and the other, as usual, in Estremadura. But the Republican armies' initiatives did not go beyond the limits of weak attacks – quite inferior to what they might have been – which managed to divert only a small contingent of the Nationalist forces engaged in the north. Thus Franco's advance into the heart of Catalunya progressed rapidly, and could not be stopped. Barcelona did not emulate Madrid in the latter's resistance. Its fall was rapid; with the army in full retreat, the government, parties and populace withdrew toward the French border. When on February 10, 1939 the Nationalist troops reached the

Below, a group of citizens from Irún arrive in French territory after ferrying across the Bidussoa River. Throughout the war, France was the natural refuge for those who tried to escape the Francoist advance. The first months of 1939 saw a desperate race by many refugees toward the French border, both by land and by sea. Left, Generals Yagüe and Asensio enter Barcelona at the head of their troops.

border, about 400,000 refugees had already crossed it.

While the Republic lay in agony, in Burgos, the provisional capital of the Nationalist zone, Franco's victories enormously consolidated his power. After January 1938, the Caudillo had substituted the Junta Técnica with a true government, the first one of his regime. It already presented the essential traits that would characterize his successive governments. Besides their common membership in the one existing party, the ministers had been chosen above all on the basis of their reliable support of the dictator. The ministers were chosen in a well-balanced selection from among the "families" of Francoism (Falangists, Carlists, Alfonsine monarchists, etc), but the presence of the military at all levels gave the defining touch to the government. While the party was relegated to a marginal role in the organizational phase, it was this executive branch, strictly controlled by Franco (particularly through his brother-in-law, Serrano Suñer, who was appointed to the Ministry of the Interior) that administered the country. But above all, the executive branch dedicated itself to "purging" the country of its enemies. With Catalunya occupied, and with final victory in sight, it issued a Law on Political Responsibilities, which became instrumental in persecuting in various ways all those who had militated in left-wing

After arriving in France, Spanish Republican refugees were gathered in concentration camps (here at Bram, 1939) and kept in conditions fit for prisoners of war.
© Sergi i Octavi Centelles

parties, or had collaborated in any form with the Popular Front governments after the Asturias revolution in October of 1934.

Franco in April 1939.
© Publifoto

The losers' camp presented a sorrowful spectacle. Some of those who had fled to France – President Azaña, who resigned; Giral; General Rojo – refused to go to the central zone. In the eyes of those who continued to resist, they were rats abandoning a sinking ship. But although no one nourished any more hope in the European war; no one – not even Negrín – saw how near it was. So everyone ran about frantically, trying to gain the best terms of surrender. Negrín first mentioned three conditions for surrender – the country's independence from any foreign hegemony, an institutional plebiscite, and guarantee against reprisals; but he ended up demanding only the latter. His adversaries hoped to obtain better conditions by getting rid of him and the Communists. The latter were the only ones to insist on resistance to the bitter end; but, as Togliatti noted in his writ-

THE LAW ON POLITICAL RESPONSIBILITIES

The Law on Political Responsibilities issued by Franco in February 1939, besides being a measure meant to persecute, was an authentic judicial monstrosity, in that it retroactively (from October 1934 on) punished as crimes actions which at the time committed had been completely legal. As can be seen from the following list included in the law, it was above all an instrument for purging.

"Article 4. Individuals to whom the following cases or circumstances are ascribed must be held politically responsible and will be subject to sanctions imposed on them in trials held against them:

... Held directorial responsibility in one of the parties, groups or associations belonging to the so-called Popular Front, or in parties or groups allied or associated with it, or in separatist organizations, or any organization opposing the victory of the National Movement.

... Occupied posts or carried out missions of a political or administrative nature, on behalf of the Popular Front government.

... Publicly proclaimed approval of the Popular Front or associate parties... or contributed to their support with financial aid.

... Called elections for representatives of the Cortes in the year 1936, was a member of the government presiding over them, or occupied posts of high responsibility during the government's existence.

... Remained abroad after July 18, 1936, without reaching national territory within a maximum term of two months." ■

MICE IN A TRAP

The last days of the Republic saw an anguished race toward the sea. A rumor was abroad: it was hoped that several English and French ships could take aboard those who were fleeing the revenge of the victors. Most of those desperate souls crowded into Alicante, the biggest port and the one furthest from the Nationalist advance. Thousands of men gathered among the abandoned wharves, where no vessel moored. They were alone or with their families, most of them without anything except their clothing. The futile wait, the death of hope, led to scenes of pain and madness. Here are some of them, as reconstructed by a Spanish historian.

"The people squeezing onto the docks of Alicante were of varying condition, but they shared a common fate, and they were shaken by the same waves of extreme discouragement. Discouragement could change into cheery optimism, on hearing a rumor or a piece of news, whether true or false. Those who were there say that the weather was cold, as if the city had wanted to deny its famed winter mildness. During the night bonfires were lit, around which the fugitives warmed themselves and dozed off. Their hopes were dashed again and again. At a given moment, a list was formed for immediate boarding; those who enviously saw others form a separate group preparing to occupy a place on the imaginary ship "about to arrive," felt their frustration grow stronger and stronger...

"There is no doubt that in the port of Alicante, there were a high number of suicides. All the witnesses agree... A man climbed to the top of a lamp post and stayed there a long time, talking like a madman in an apocalyptic tone; some say he threw himself on the sidewalk, others that before falling, he shot himself... Some threw themselves in the sea and drowned; others repented once they were in the water, and shouted for help. Many shot themselves... The desire for suicide spread like a contagious disease." ■

– Romero, L. *El final de la guerra.* Barcelona: Ariel, 1976. 451–452.

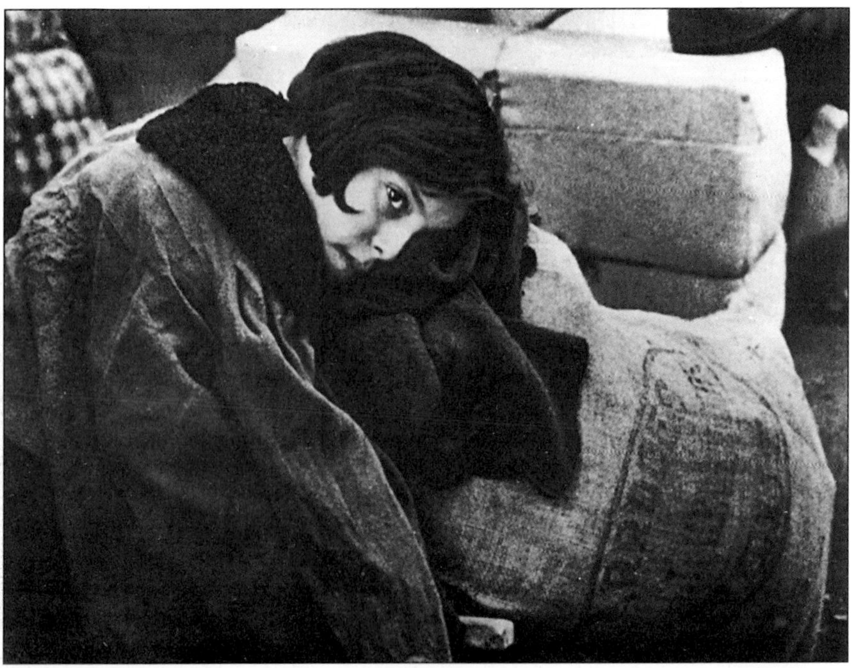

ings, they were aware of being isolated, even with respect to the populace.

Franco nearly had victory in his grasp, and would agree to nothing but unconditional surrender. At the end of January, France and England recognized his government; their foreign ministers, Bonnet and Lord Halifax, treated the ambassadors of the Republic with detachment to the point of ridicule, as they desperately tried to enlist the ministers' help in obtaining less harsh terms of surrender. These ministers did not make much of an effort, and from the Caudillo, they received nothing more than vague promises of mercy.

Given its symbolic value and the generous heroism of many of its defenders, Republican Spain did not deserve the tragic, grotesque end to which it was condemned. Certain of its military leaders, in the anguished final squeeze, could find nothing better to do than fall back on the old method of the *pronunciamiento*. On March 5, 1939, Colonel Segismundo Casado, commander of the army of the Center, with the support of Miaja, Besteiro, and the anarchist commander, Cipriano Mera, rebelled against the Negrín government. He then formed a *Consejo de defensa* (headed by Miaja), and started up combat against sectors remaining under the control of the Communist commanders. Valencia, Cartagena and above all, Madrid, became the scene of violent conflict. While Negrín and most of his ministers had now escaped abroad along with the leaders of the Communist Party, in key areas of Madrid, armed tanks began to maneuver,

In Madrid on May 18, 1939 Franco greets his troops during the parade celebrating his victory. The arduous struggle of the Republic concluded sadly, after the ignominious, old-fashioned pronunciamiento *attempted by Colonel Segismundo Casado (below). Left, a young refugee in Barcelona, in a famous photo taken by Robert Capa.*
© 3 Publifoto

lines of artillery formed, and cannon balls flew. One of Franco's spies sent a dispatch to the Caudillo's headquarters: "Chaos on the rise. Casado incapable of dominating situation. Danger disorders and massacres. Chance advantageous offensive."

But Franco was still suspicious. He knew he could enter Madrid without firing a single shot. Now that the situation was under control, Casado and Miaja's *Consejo de defensa* sent out surrender proposals with the same conditions as Negrín's. The difference was that, once the Communists were sent away or imprisoned, Franco would be more indulgent – or so it was thought. On March 28, 1938, the Nationalist troops entered Madrid amid cheering crowds, who greeted Franco, raising their arms in the

1939–1975: FRANCO'S

In modern times, no country of western Europe has known such a merciless, bloody purge as that actuated by Generalísimo Franco. A calculation of the number of death sentences carried out until the early 1950s varies from the 28,000 estimated by the Francoist historian, Salas Larrazabal, and the 150,000 indicated by the pro-Republican, Tamanes. A frightening number, at any rate, reflecting more the will to annihilate the enemy than any mere eagerness for revenge; more a continuation of the war custom of taking no prisoners, than the pursuance of any political design.

This epilogue of the war presented more a military character than a political one. In this, it presaged the dictator's regime. In fact, the dominance of the military element over the political one corresponded to Franco's mentality. While it is true that at first, the regime was a carbon copy of Fascist regimes, having the same ceremonies and the same institutional characteristics – the Caudillo at the apex of power, a single party, a corporative type of system, and so on – at the same time, as long as it lasted it was closely identified with the person of the dictator (it was called "Francoist," and not, for example, "Falangist"). It continued to be based on the constant superiority of the military element over the civilian one.

Historians have stressed Franco's capacity to keep his power constant through a divide-and-conquer strategy: that is, by playing the so-called "families" of Francoism against each other. One year, the Falangists would be in favor; another year, the Carlists, and so on through the monarchists, the Catholics, the technocrats from Opus Dei, and so on. But the military stood by each one of these; the military was not one "family" beside the others, but a reserve of reliable personnel and politico-administrative leaders within the regime. From 1941 on, the Caudillo's second-in-command, for example, was always a military man: first Admiral Carrero Blanco, then General Muñoz Grandes and finally, during the last two years of the dictatorship (1974–1975), Arias Navarro, a civilian who had led a juridical-military career.

Until 1969 the *Movimiento*, whose militia was always led by a member of the military, had as air in the fascist salute. The Generalísimo made no concessions. In chaotic flight, Republican troops and groups of the populace veered toward the Mediterranean, hoping to find ships that would evacuate them. But for many (if not for Casado, Miaja, and their men), all escape routes were closed. On April 1, Franco issued his last war bulletin: "Today, having defeated and imprisoned the Red Army, the Nationalist troops have reached their final military objectives. The war is over."

In the halls of democratic Europe, the news was greeted with little surprise. The disappearance of that Republic, which had become a threat to western Europe's value system brought a sigh of relief, when all was said and done. The leaders of those countries thought that the danger to peace had disappeared along with the Republic. It is perhaps unfair to claim that with their policy of accommodation regarding Spain, those leaders encouraged Hitler to wage war. But it is certain that as far as peace went, they were wrong.

Franco in 1974, with a young Juan Carlos de Bourbon. Thirty-nine years, one month and twenty days separate October 1, 1936, when Franco was appointed Head of State, from November 20, 1975, the day of the dictator's death. Thirteen months after he died, approval of the referendum on the Law for Political Reform laid down the legal basis for dismantling the Francoist state and democratizing the country under the aegis of a constitutional monarchy.

REGIME IN PERSPECTIVE

its secretary a military man still in active service. In the 36 years during which the regime lasted, the Ministry of the Interior was occupied for 32 years by a member of the military. The provincial governors (or prefects) were often military men as well, especially in the main cities.

Many technical and administrative tasks were assigned to the army; for 24 years the head of the Ministry of Industry was a general. But the army was the regime's supporting column above all in the maintenance of social order, and in the administration of justice. The police corps was militarized; the majority of functionaries in the Ministry of the Interior were military men in active service. Any form of turbulence in public law and order, beginning with strikes, was considered a crime to be pursued by military justice. Won over to fascism (like many members of the military between the two world wars), and influenced in the formation of his regime by demonstrations of power on the part of the forces that had helped him win the war, Franco wore fascism as if it were a suit of clothes, without embracing it with his most intimate convictions. He grasped its innovative elements only in a practical sense, in order to stay in power. He would not let himself be overcome by ideology, and preserved only the dictatorial essence of a fascist regime by maintaining a kind of neo-absolutism.

This explains why his dictatorship was able to survive the fall of other fascisms, and why it managed to be more open to change than a truly fascist regime. So much so that, upon the dictator's death, a bloodless passage to a wholly different kind of government took place: democracy.

The Generalísimo, renouncing any totalitarian ambitions, had delegated ethics, customs and the education of youth to the Church, and now the Church had changed many of its attitudes. The army's interventionist inclinations had also changed a great deal, with the advent of a new generation. With these changes, Spanish society had gradually been permeated by modern and democratic tendencies.

So it was not surprising, nor did it appear to be an improbable transformation, when the last secretary of the *Movimiento*, Adolfo Suárez, became one of the principal authors of democratization. ■

Bibliography

■ Alpert, M. El ejército de la república en la guerra civil. Barcelona, 1978.

■ Azaña, Manuel. *Obras Completas.* Mexico, 1966–68.

■ Bolloten, B. *The Grand Camouflage.* London, 1968

■ Brenan, G. *The Spanish Labyrinth: An Account of the Social and Political Background of the Civil War.* Cambridge, 1991.

■ Carr, R. *The Republic and the Civil War in Spain.* London, 1971.

■ Carroll, P. *The Odyssey of the American Lincoln Brigade: Americans in the Spanish Civil War.* Palo Alto, 1994.

■ Fraser, R. *Blood of Spain: An Oral History of the Spanish Civil War.* New York, 1979.

■ Gallo, M. *Spain Under Franco.* London, 1973.

■ Ibarruri, D. *They Shall Not Pass: The Autobiography of La Pasionaria.* London, 1967.

■ Jackson, G. *A Concise History of the Civil War.* New York, 1974.

■ Kaminski, H. *Ceux de Barcelone.* Paris, 1937.

■ Kaplan, T. *Anarchists of Andalusia, 1868–1903.* Princeton, 1977.

■ Koltsov, M. *Diario de la guerra de España.* Paris, 1963.

■ Malefakis, E. *Agrarian Reform and Peasant Revolution in Spain.* New Haven, 1970.

■ Orwell, G. *Homage to Catalonia.* Boston, 1959.

■ Preston, P. *The Coming of the Spanish Civil War, 1931–1936.* London, 1978.

■ Ranzato, G. *Rivoluzione e guerra civile in Spagna. 1931–1939.* Turin, 1975.

■ Ranzato, G. *Guerre fratricide. Le guerre civili in età contemporanea.* Turin, 1994.

■ Thomas, H. *The Spanish Civil War.* Harmondsworth, 1997.

■ Trotsky, L. *The Spanish Revolution (1931–1939).* New York, 1973.

■ Tussell, J. *Franco en la guerra civil. Una biografía política.* Madrid, 1992.

Chronology

1923 General Miguel Primo de Rivera sets up a dictatorship with the consensus of King Alfonso XIII. He is acclaimed by many as a "man of order" capable of "regenerating" the country, but his popularity decreases until he finally leaves the country in 1930.

1931 In the administrative elections of **April 12** the Republicans and Socialists defeat the monarchist parties. On **April 14** the Republic is proclaimed. Alfonso XIII leaves Spain. A provisional government is formed, headed by Alcalá Zamora. On **May 10 and 11** there are episodes of anticlericalism, with the burning of churches and convents. On **June 28** the elections for the Cortes confirm support for Republicans and socialists. The Republican Azaña is appointed head of a government in which the socialist Caballero is Labor Minister. On **December 9** the new constitution is approved: Article 26 imposes harsh conditions on the Church, including a prohibition against teaching.

1932 In **January** the anarchists organize insurrections throughout the country. On **August 10** a coup d'état, organized by General Sanjurjo, fails. In **September** an agrarian reform law is approved. A statute for Catalunya is approved setting up a regional parliament (Generalitat) in charge of controlling local finances.

1933 In **January** the anarchist trade union, CNT, proclaims a general strike. anarchist riots break out in Catalunya and in some Andalusian villages. The government is defeated in elections of constitutional court members; Azaña resigns. On **October 9** the Cortes is dissolved and new elections are held. On **October 29** José Antonio Primo di Rivera founds the Falange in Madrid. On **November 19** the center-right parties win the elections: the new government is headed by Alejandro Lerroux.

1934 On **April 11** the Generalitat passes a law on agrarian contracts in Catalunya, which is vetoed by the constitutional court on **June 9**. Between **June 5 and 11**, several strikes in the Andalusia and Estremadura countryside fail. On **October 4** Lerroux reforms the government, turning control of three ministries over to Gil Robles' right-wing Catholic party, CEDA. On **October 6**, an insurrection organized by the left breaks out in Madrid and Asturias; at the same time, in Catalunya, an independence revolt breaks out. The uprising immediately fails everywhere, except in Asturias. Eventually, even that revolt is crushed by Franco, with the help of the African army he brought from Morocco.

1935 On **March 1** a new agrarian law annuls the effects of the earlier reforms. On **May 17** Franco is appointed head of the chiefs of staff. Dissension within the center-right coalition causes an irremediable crisis.

1936 On **January 7** the parliament is dissolved. On **January 15** the left-wing parties sign the electoral pact of the Popular Front. On **February 16** the Popular Front wins the elections by a small margin, but the electoral law allows it a wide majority of seats.

1936 On **February 19** the Azaña government is formed: one of its first measures is the liberation of prisoners taken during the events of October 1934. On **March 15** the Falange is declared illegal and José Antonio is arrested. On **April 7** the parliament removes Alcalá Zamora from power as president, and on **May 10** Azaña is elected the new president. Two days later, a new government is formed, headed by Casares Quiroga. On **July 13** the monarchist leader, Calvo Sotelo, is assassinated in reprisal for the assassination of Lieutenant Castillo, a leftist sympathizer. On **July 17** the

African army rebels; in the days immediately following, other garrisons on the peninsula rebel; the coup d'état fails, but the rebel generals (in particular Mola, Queipo de Llano, Cabanellas and Franco) refuse any mediation with the government. The coup forces form a national defense junta, headed by Cabanellas. After attempts at negotiation fail, the government is turned over to José Giral, but the authority of his central government is strongly limited by the autonomous juntas and councils that are springing up across the country, in reaction to the attempted coup. On **July 28**, German and Italian aviation forces begin to set up an airlift between Morocco and Seville; after landing on the peninsula, the Nationalist troops begin to move the offensive northward. On **August 2** France proposes "non-intervention": Germany and Italy agree formally, but in fact continue to help the rebels. On **September 4** Largo Caballero takes over as head of a government uniting all the Popular Front forces. The same day, the rebels occupy Talavera, and on **September 26**, reach Toledo, breaking off the siege of the Alcazár. On **September 30**, in Burgos, the defense junta publishes a decree (dated the preceding day) appointing Franco Head of State and Commander-in-Chief. In **October** the first Soviet aid to the Republicans arrives in Cartagena. On **November 4** the anarchists enter the Caballero government. On **November 7**, the government moves to Valencia, far from the front. In the battle of Madrid (**November 8–23**), the International Brigades undergo fire for the first time. Franco's strike against the capital is thrown back.

1937 On **February 10** the Nationalist army (with Italian aid) occupies Malaga, but fails in successive attempts to attack Madrid: it is defeated in the battle of Jarama (**February 6–15**) and again in the battle of Guadalajara (**March 8–18**). The Madrid stalemate lasts for two years. Franco moves toward the Basque country and on **April 26** bombs Guérnica. Between **May 3 and 8** Barcelona is the scene of street battles between communists and Catalan separatists on one side, and the anarchists and the POUM on the other. On **May 17** the Negrín government is formed, which excludes the anarchists and dissolves the POUM. Between **May 29 and 31**, the German cruiser *Deutschland* bombards Ibiza and Almeria. On **June 3** General Mola dies in an airplane accident. On **June 19** Bilbao falls. Four days later, Franco abolishes the Basque autonomy statute. The Republicans start up the battles of Brunete (**July 7–26**) and Belchite (**August**) without gaining any substantial results. On **October 31** the Republican government moves to Barcelona.

1938 In **March** the *Fuero del Trabajo* is published. On **March 9** the Nationalist offensive in Aragon begins; by **April 15** they reach the Mediterranean, breaking the Republican territory in two. At the **end of April** Lérida and Balaguer fall. On **July 19** the Republicans start the battle of the Ebro. On **August 26** Santander falls. On **November 15** the Republicans retreat from the Ebro front. The International Brigades leave Spain as a sign of the Negrín government's willingness to reach a peaceful compromise. On **December 23** the Nationalists unleash a new offensive against Catalunya.

1939 On **January 26** Barcelona falls. The government, army and populace try to flee toward the French border. On **February 1** the last session of the Republican Cortes is held at Figueras, near the border. On **February 12** Negrín and his government re-enter Madrid. On **February 13** Franco enacts the Law on Political Responsibilities. On **February 27** France and England recognize the Francoist government of Burgos. Azaña resigns. On **March 5**, Colonel Casado breaks up the Negrín government, hoping to gain from Franco better peace conditions. On **March 28** the Nationalists enter Madrid. On **April 1** Franco announces the surrender of the Republican army.

Index of names

The Traveller's History Series

A Traveller's History of Australia	*$14.95/£8.99 pb*
A Traveller's History of the Caribbean	*$14.95/£8.99 pb*
A Traveller's History of China	*$14.95/£7.99 pb*
A Traveller's History of England	*$14.95/£8.99 pb*
A Traveller's History of France	*$14.95/£8.99 pb*
A Traveller's History of Greece	*$14.95/£7.95 pb*
A Traveller's History of India	*$14.95/£8.99 pb*
A Traveller's History of Ireland	*$14.95/£7.95 pb*
A Traveller's History of Italy	*$14.95/£8.99 pb*
A Traveller's History of Japan	*$14.95/£8.99 pb*
A Traveller's History of London	*$14.95/£8.99 pb*
A Traveller's History of North Africa	*$14.95/£8.99 pb*
A Traveller's History of Paris	*$14.95/£8.99 pb*
A Traveller's History of Russia	*$14.95/£7.95 pb*
A Traveller's History of Scotland	*$14.95/£8.99 pb*
A Traveller's History of Spain	*$14.95/£8.99 pb*
A Traveller's History of Turkey	*$14.95/£8.99 pb*
A Traveller's History of the USA	*$14.95/£8.99 pb*

Available at good bookshops everywhere
We encourage you to support your local bookseller

To order or request a full list of titles
please contact us at one of the addresses listed below:

In the US:
Interlink Publishing Group, Inc.
46 Crosby Street
Northampton, MA 01060
Tel: 800-238-LINK/Fax: 413-582-7057
e-mail: interpg@aol.com
website: www.interlinkbooks.com

In the UK:
Windrush Press Ltd.
Little Window, High Street
Moreton-in-Marsh
Gloucestershire GL56 0LL
Tel: 01608 652012/Fax 01608 652125
email: info@windrushpress.com
website: www.windrushpress.com